The Social Psychology of Organizing

KARL E. WEICK
University of Minnesota

ADDISON-WESLEY PUBLISHING COMPANY
Reading, Massachusetts
Menlo Park, California • London • Don Mills, Ontario

TOPICS IN SOCIAL PSYCHOLOGY
Charles A. Kiesler, Yale University, Series Editor

Foreword

It is becoming increasingly difficult for anyone to be a generalist in social psychology. Not only is the number of articles published zooming, but new researchable areas of interest are multiplying as well. A researcher finds more fascinating topics these days than he used to, but he also finds himself behind in his reading of all but one or two of them. As a result, the quality of the broad introductory book in social psychology has suffered. No one can any longer be an expert in all of social psychology.

As an alternative, we offer the present series, *Topics in Social Psychology,* directed toward the student with no prior background in social psychology. Taken as a whole, the series adequately covers the field of social psychology, but it has the advantage that each short book was written by an expert in the area. The instructor can select some subset of the books to make up his course, the particular subset depending on his biases and inclinations. In addition, the individual volumes can be useful in several ways: as supplementary reading in, perhaps, a sociology course; to introduce more advanced courses (for example, a graduate seminar in attitude change); or just for peeking at recent developments in social psychology.

Karl Weick's contribution to the series centers on the psychology of organizing—when and why people do it. In a sense, this is an old, but central problem of social psychology. However, Weick offers a fresh theoretical approach that provides us oldsters with new insights while maintaining the proper level of difficulty for an introductory text.

Charles A. Kiesler

iii

Acknowledgment

In a recent article by William Gass* there is a stunning sentence. It reads, "Nonpersons unperson persons." Therein lies the drama of this book. The thinking and writing necessary to produce it transformed me into a nonperson, potentially capable of unpersoning those around me who really matter. Fortunately, they were stubborn enough that I couldn't pull it off. I would like to mention a few of these "stubborn" people to whom I'm grateful. Harold Pepinsky has been my durable confidant, critic, and constructive force, and his light touch permeates everything. My students have been more tolerant of intellectual "flings" and more active participants in them than I had any right to expect. The National Science Foundation through Grant GS 1927 has provided the support and understanding for much of the theorizing in this book with minimal interference. Finally, the person most stubborn about being unpersoned has been my secretary, Mrs. Barbara Bailey. Her tolerance is staggering, and her success in making me "look good" at some of the most absurd moments is awesome.

But there is one final group of people who led me to rewrite Gass's words. Persons reperson nonpersons. And that's just what Karen, Kirk, Kyle, and Kris did. They took the fragments left after a bout of writing, reassembled them, and gently nudged me back to the typewriter. In return all they asked of me was, "How's the book going?" Without their love I could never have answered, "Great!"

---

*W. H. Gass, "The Artist and Society," *The New Republic, 159,* No. 4 (1968), pp. 16-19.

Contents

CHAPTER ONE

What Organizing Looks Like

This book does not cover (that can be read as either "include" or "conceal") organization theory, and its purpose is not to instruct. Instead, its purpose is to tell the reader something about how he can learn about organizations. It does not tell him what organizations are, for a very simple reason. Organizations and their environments change so rapidly that it is unrealistic to show what they are like now, because that's not the way they're going to be later. Rather than burden the reader with dated information—information that assumes an unchanging environment—my purpose is to sensitize the reader to ways of looking at and thinking about organizations. The reader's responsibility is to do the learning; my responsibility is to tell him how to go about it. The concepts, criticisms, and viewpoints discussed in this book are intended to prod the reader toward elaboration, disproof, or further associations.

If you're going to learn about organizations, it is not necessary that you assume immediately that they are complex ("the currently popular term *complex organizations* conveys more information about organization theorists than about organization"; Weick, 1965, p. 204), or that they differ from groups of smaller size. Instead, assume that there are processes which create, maintain, and dissolve social collectivities, that these processes constitute the work of organizing, and that the ways in which these processes are continuously executed *are* the organization. The same processes operate through a variety of media; they are expressed through whatever props and people are at hand, but they remain basically the same processes. Their appearance may change, but their workings do not. Thus, if you wanted to learn something about an organization, you might look for "interlocked behaviors that are embedded in conditionally related processes." The argument of this book is that if you could observe, describe, and summarize conceptually the features in the preceding phrase, then you would know a great deal about organizations. Obviously, that phrase, as it stands, is too cryptic to be of any help; it will be given substance later. For the moment, we simply want to provide some idea of the way we will talk about organizations. You can see how this way of talking and learning departs from standard treatments of organization if you read a more conventional and complete description of what an organization is: "An organization is the rational coordination of the activities of a number of people for the achievement of some common, explicit purpose or goal, through division of labor and function and through a hierarchy of authority and responsibility" (Schein, 1965, p. 8). The reader should keep this latter definition in mind because it is representative of current ways of thinking about organizations; it contains properties which most people regard as crucial for an understanding of organizations, and which many regard as constituting the uniqueness of organizations.

The following sections illustrate the process and consequences of organizing.

ORGANIZING: THE EMERGENCE OF "MAJORITY RULE"

Piet Hein's aphoristic poem (or "grook") entitled "Majority Rule" tells us a great deal about how organizing occurs.

> His party was the Brotherhood of Brothers,
> and there were more of them than of the others.
> That is, they constituted that minority
> which formed the greater part of the majority.
> Within the party, he was of the faction
> that was supported by the greater fraction.
> And in each group, within each group, he sought
> the group that could command the most support.
> The final group had finally elected
> a triumvirate whom they all respected.
> Now of these three, two had the final word,
> because the two could overrule the third.
> One of these two was relatively weak,
> so one alone stood at the final peak.
> He was THE GREATER NUMBER of the pair
> which formed the most part of the three that were
> elected by the most of those whose boast
> it was to represent the most of most

of most of most of the entire state—
or of the most of it at any rate.
He never gave himself a moment's slumber
but sought the welfare of the greatest number.
And all the people, everywhere they went,
knew to their cost exactly what it meant
to be dictated to by the majority.
But that meant nothing—they were the minority.[1]

One way to understand the events portrayed in this poem is to transform them into an organizational chart. It is common practice to depict organizations graphically and to regard the lines in the chart as indicating such things as communication relationships, lines of authority, chain of command, levels within the organization, superior-subordinate relationships, etc. A simplified organization chart for "Majority Rule" is found in Fig. 1. The numbers attached to each level are arbitrary, and the labels at each level correspond to the labels used in the poem. If we look at the chart, we can see several interesting features. For example, note the direction of the arrows. In most charts they would point from the top to the bottom, yet in this case they point in the reverse direction. This is partly because we are discussing the *process* of organizing and how organization emerges. Our discussion is consistent with the sizable literature (e.g., Cohen and Bennis, 1961) that talks about the emergence of leadership and demonstrates that this emergence is viewed as more or less legitimate depending on the extent to which members participate in selecting the leader. The arrows in the chart, however, make an even more important point. They imply that subordinates ultimately determine the amount of influence exerted by those who lead. This is a prominent theme in organization theory (e.g., Mechanic, 1964; Read, 1962; Blau, 1954, 1959). The argument is presented in perhaps the clearest form by Barnard:

> If a directive communication is accepted by one to whom it is addressed, its authority for him is confirmed or established. It is admitted as the basis of action. Disobedience of such a communication is a denial of its authority for him. Therefore, under this definition the decision as to whether an order has authority or not lies with the persons to whom it is addressed, and does not reside in "persons of authority" or those who issue orders. . . . Our definition of authority . . . no doubt will appear to many whose eyes are fixed only on enduring organizations to be a platform of chaos. And so it is—exactly so in the preponderance of attempted organizations. They fail because they can maintain no authority, that is,

---

[1] From Piet Hein, *Grooks* (Cambridge, Mass.: M.I.T. Press, 1966), p. 22. Reprinted by permission.

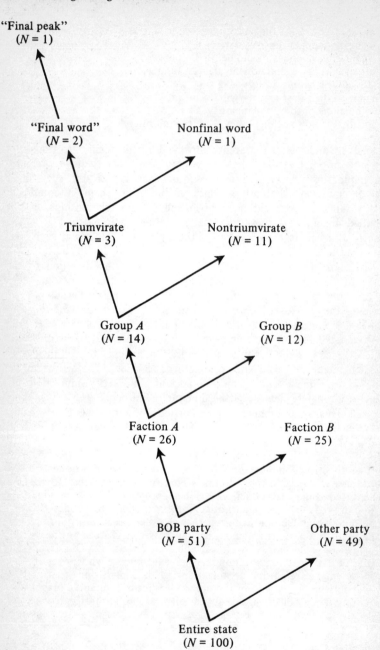

Fig. 1

they cannot secure sufficient contributions of personal efforts to be effective or cannot induce them on terms that are efficient. In the last analysis the authority fails because the individuals in sufficient numbers regard the burden involved in accepting necessary order as changing the balance of advantage against their interest, and they withdraw or withhold the indispensable contributions.[2]

This quotation suggests several additional properties of the grook: (1) the person at the top is in a vulnerable position; (2) subordinates often do not realize the amount of control they actually have—an observation that occurs repeatedly in experiments on coalition formation (e.g., Vinacke, *et al.,* 1966); (3) if the hierarchy is to be maintained, it must be continuously reestablished by the person above's sending *acceptable* orders to the person below (in Barnard's language, orders must be within the "Zone of Indifference" for subordinates; 1938, p. 167); (4) the acceptance of orders is always determined in part by self-interest (not only do orders vary in their acceptability, but subordinates vary in their interests and definitions of what is acceptable).

As a sidelight on the issue of authority, it is interesting to note that even though there are seven levels in our chart, the last three levels involve the *same* three people in different combinations. Three are picked to rule; of these three two can override the third; and one of the two is weak, so one person winds up in actual control. The crucial property here is that effective influence in the large collectivity depends on alliances among a very few members. Several theorists describe organizational functioning in terms of alliances that are established (e.g., Caplow, 1964; Cyert and March, 1963). These theorists argue that to understand an organization is to locate the crucial alliances that control large numbers of people. This is precisely the point made by the grook. Despite the apparent size of this group ($N = 100$) and despite the fact that there are supposedly 100 different influential people, in reality the crucial decisions—those thought to be the *majority* decisions—are made by one man. The important point is not that one man rules; rather it is the fact that this control is made possible by the pattern of alliances that exists in the group. It is the pattern of relationships, *not* the traits of the individuals *per se,* that makes it possible for influence to be concentrated.

Although control relationships are regarded by many as the key element for understanding the organization (e.g., Bennis, 1959; Scott *et al.,* 1967; Tannenbaum, 1968), there are other features commonly discussed in organization theory that are visible in the grook. For instance, the number of

---

[2]From C. I. Barnard, *The Functions of the Executive* (Cambridge, Mass.: Harvard Univ. Press, 1938), pp. 163-165. Reprinted by permission.

levels present in an organization (seven levels are depicted in the example) is regarded by many theorists as a crucial property that explains much of organizational functioning (e.g., Porter and Lawler, 1965; Evan, 1963). This property is commonly referred to as flat versus tall organizations. There are several reasons why this dimension is judged important. For example, levels determine the number of subordinates that report to a given supervisor. If we hold the size of the organization constant, the fewer the number of levels, the greater the number of subordinates who report to a single supervisor, the less closely can the supervisor monitor his subordinates, and the more autonomy they have to make their own decisions. Thus the structural variable of tall versus flat has the important psychological consequence of determining the closeness and frequency with which any member can be supervised; this in turn affects his feelings of freedom versus coercion. Generally, it is posited that the more self-determination allowed to the worker, the higher his productivity and satisfaction (e.g., Blauner, 1960; Katz, 1964).

The distinction between tall and flat organizations also affects communication. In general, the relationship is that the flatter the organization, the less likely it is that communication will become distorted, since there are fewer decision points through which it passes before it reaches the unit that must take action. Phrased in a converse form, the rule is this: the greater the number of people through whom a communication must pass, the greater the likelihood that communication will be transformed. (March and Simon, 1958, label this "uncertainty absorption"; some idea of its mechanics can be found in Campbell, 1958.)

From another point of view, it is possible to interpret tall versus flat in terms of another venerable concept in organization theory, the informal organization. Informal organization consists of the interaction patterns that develop in addition to those that are formally prescribed by lines of authority (Carzo and Yanouzas, 1967, Chap. 5). The relevance of the informal organization to the present discussion is that as organizations become flatter and as supervision becomes less direct, it is probable that a greater number of informal contacts will be initiated and maintained, and that these contacts will have a more substantial effect on performance. When supervision is less frequent and less direct, informal contacts may be initiated for the purpose of getting work done (Blau, 1954). In other words, assistance cannot be counted on from a supervisor to whom several persons report, hence this support is sought at a parallel level from those who are engaged in similar activities. Added impetus for these informal alignments comes from the fact that the supervisor in his role of helper also sooner or later assumes the role of evaluator. He judges the output of the subordinates and bases his promotion and demotion decisions on these assessments. This means that the supervisor plays an extremely complicated role. Subordinates are hesitant to ask for assistance from the supervisor because of their belief that this will reveal their incompetence and will affect subsequent decisions about salary and promotion.

The major point to be drawn from this is that organizations vary in their number of levels, and that the number of levels directly affects supervision, communication, and informal alliances, and indirectly produces psychological consequences. Some additional features of our grook can be recognized. The fact that there is considerable separation between the leader and the members of the "entire state" can be demonstrated in terms of the following sentence: "He never gave himself a moment's slumber but sought the welfare of the greatest number." If we substitute the word "greater" for the word "greatest," the problem becomes apparent. For this sentence can mean the leader sought the welfare of himself, of his partner and himself, of the ruling triumvirate, of the group, of the faction, of the BOB party, or of the entire state. Note that the coalition partner, the ruling triumvirate, and the group are closer in proximity to him than are the state or the BOB party. This suggests the possibility that the more remote the level, the greater the likelihood that its welfare will be ignored in decisions, and the more immediate the level, the more its welfare will control decisions. This is related to the discussion of communication distortion mentioned above. The claims of adjacent levels can be apprehended more accurately than those of more remote levels.

Because organizations are basically orderly, it is often argued that a prominent feature of them is that members are replaceable or substitutable (e.g., Deutsch, 1949). This ties in with the broader notion that organizations are contrived plans for the execution of complex tasks. Stated in another way, only parts of persons are actually used in an organization (Steiner, 1955). As long as the person performs his portion of the assigned task, his performance is judged satisfactory. More crucial is the fact that because his function is specified, it is possible to replace him with another person so long as the newcomer is capable of performing the same portion of the same task with the same degree of skill. If we reexamine the grook in the light of this fact, it is apparent that substitutability is more difficult to accomplish the higher one goes in the hierarchy. If a person is substituted for a present member at the party or state level, there should be little effect on the state of affairs depicted in Fig. 1, since the tasks performed at these levels are fairly simple. But if a member of the "ruling triumvirate" is replaced, there is a greater likelihood that the relationships will change.

Most organization theorists assume that organizing is done in order to promote goal attainment (e.g., Etzioni, 1964, pp. 5-19). This emphasis was apparent in Schein's definition stated earlier. But a goal is not readily apparent in the grook unless we wish to speculate that something as nebulous as "survival," "attainment of welfare," or "attainment of control over the environment" is the "reason" why these people united. This would seem to stretch unduly the information contained in the grook. This point should not be dismissed, because in subsequent chapters it will be argued that organizing is *not* necessarily an attempt to attain some specified goal. The absence of a goal in the grook makes it *more,* rather than less, like an organization.

In the grook, one gets the impression that first organizing occurred, then *after* it was concluded the reason for the organizing became apparent. It is as if the persons acted so that they could eventually determine what it was that they had done. This sequence in which actions *precede* goals may well be a more accurate portrait of organizational functioning. The common assertion that goal consensus must occur prior to action obscures the fact that consensus is impossible unless there is something tangible around which it can occur. And this "something tangible" may well turn out to be actions *already completed*. Thus it is entirely possible that goals statements are retrospective rather than prospective.

Since any organization theory has to specify why members consent to join and remain in organizations, most theories discuss the "social contract" that is implicit in organizational membership (e.g., Barnard, 1948, pp. 113-118; Thompson, 1967, Chap. 8). Schein designates this contract as a psychological contract and describes it this way: "The notion of a psychological contract implies that the individual has a variety of expectations of the organization and that the organization has a variety of expectations of him. These expectations not only cover how much work is to be performed for how much pay, but also involve the whole pattern of rights, privileges, and obligations between worker and organization" (1965, p. 11). It should be noted that implicit in the concept of the contract is the notion that there is an exchange of commodities, and it is this feature of the contract which has been given considerable prominence in writings about organization (e.g., Whyte, 1959). Satisfaction, productivity, interpersonal ties, and the likelihood of leaving are all dependent on the terms of the contract and its fate at any given moment in time. What is demonstrated in the grook is perhaps the most basic form in which a contract exists. Individual members consent to be governed, in return for which some smaller body agrees to govern in a beneficent manner. Phrased in terms of the grook, the majority consents to become the minority in the belief that their interests are more likely to be promoted.

One way to contrast small groups and large organizations is to view the latter as a group of groups (e.g., Simon, 1957). This feature is illustrated in the grook and affords the wedge by which additional psychological concepts become relevant for organization theory. Two such relevant notions are link pins (people with membership in two or more overlapping groups who promote cooperation between the separate groups) and ethnocentrism (ingroup loyalty coupled with outgroup deprecation). If one views an organization as a group of groups, this implies that there may be some competition among the several groups for scarce resources (Bass and Dunteman, 1963; Sherif and Sherif, 1964, pp. 224-244; Campbell, 1967). This competition often leads members to overrate the virtues of their own group and downgrade those of other groups (Campbell, 1967; Merton, 1940). These divisive forces are often reduced when one or more members hold joint membership in or are acceptable to both groups (Likert, 1961; Heiskanen,

1967). Presumably, the "excluded groups" on the right-hand side of Fig. 1 would exhibit some hostility toward the groups in the left-hand portion. The groups on the left control the scarce resource of power, which has been removed from the control of the members on the right-hand side. The left-hand members themselves would probably have their own hostilities—toward the people in "higher" ingroups. Working against this tendency of excluded members to deprecate "included members" are the facts that there are link pins and that all groups may share the goal of leading a good life. To the extent that all groups share this goal despite their differences, and to the extent that they believe the leader is capable of improving their state, then intergroup hostility should decrease.

Anyone who samples the literature on organizations will soon notice a term that occurs over and over again, "rationality." This concept does not necessarily mean that organizational actions are logical or sensible, but rather that they are intended, thought about, planned, calculated, or designed for a purpose. The emphasis is on the idea that what happens in an organization was at one point in time expected or planned to happen. The fact that organizations typically exhibit a great deal of turbulence, disorder, and unpredictability does not necessarily disprove the theory that their *origins* were rational or that they are trying to be rational.

The grook, rather than demonstrating rationality as such, shows the trouble one has in trying to apply this concept. If there is "calculation" or "intent" present in the grook, the only person to whom this might safely be attributed is the person on top. If "rationality" is used this way, it means an expedient set of alliances composed for the ultimate purpose of gaining control. Rationality lies in the several means that were used to achieve the final goal of gaining control. We could say that the other members tacitly "consented" to this rational plan; but if we do this, we lose the force of the concept.

To avoid this problem of the concept's becoming meaningless, one alternative is to adopt a convention suggested by Simon (1957, pp. 33-41)—the concept of "bounded rationality." The essence of this notion is that individuals have perceptual as well as information-processing limits, and even though they may intend to act rationally, they can do so only in a limited fashion. This limited fashion consists of acting on the basis of sufficient knowledge rather than complete knowledge (the concept of satisficing), of using simple, unlaborious rules to search for a solution when a problem arises (e.g., searching in the immediate vicinity of the problem), and of using shortcuts whenever possible. In terms of bounded rationality, we could say that the persons in the grook facilitated the form of control that finally emerged; when faced with decisions they used simple decision rules (e.g., the majority wins) and applied a criterion of sufficiency (e.g., "if this agreement will enable us to get on with our work, let's accept it"), and there was little review of all possible consequences. The members dealt with "here and now" and did so in the way that involved the least possible effort. While some of us may balk at this unflattering portrait of mankind, to do so is to miss the point being made. The point is that *if* one assumes that the actors have limited rationality, then it follows that decisions will be made in terms of localized disturbances to which abbreviated analyses will be applied, with short-term recommendations as the result. A search for more stable solutions (i.e., those which will solve the problem once and for all) is unlikely; consequences are not given much attention, and apparently logical solutions may prove faulty as their consequences ramify. Furthermore, since the consequences of a decision often occur much later than the decision itself, it is difficult for the members to trace backward from these disruptive consequences to determine precisely what caused them. The members cannot make such an analysis simply because there are too many competing explanations. Thus, all the members can do when a new problem arises is to engage in more localized problem-solving.

What all this suggests is that rationality is best understood as in the eye of the beholder. It is *his* aims and how he consciously sets out to accomplish them that constitute the clearest, most easily specified component of rationality. To say that "systems" or organizations engage in rational decision-making makes sense only if we can specify some set of persons who agree on some desired outcome, on a specified set of means to attain this outcome, on ways in which the specific means will be activated, and on how it will be known whether the desired outcome was attained or not. Since this fourfold agreement is more difficult when large numbers of persons are involved, it is likely that rationality will characterize mostly small groups of actors and that, at any moment in time, organizations will have several different and contradictory rationalities.

The persistence of the concept of rationality in the organizational literature, however, is not surprising. It is not surprising partly because organization theory has its root in economic theory, and rationality is a prominent concept in economic models of man (e.g., Latane, 1963). But the persistence of this concept also shows that theorists are simply human beings. Cognitive theorists have repeatedly demonstrated that when people try to make sense out of events, they are aided most in doing this if they can establish motivational reasons for the actions (e.g., Heider, 1958; Schutz, 1967). That is, we know more about a person if we can observe him and say, "Oh, *that's* what he's *trying* to do." When we can say this, we have a plausible, motivational explanation of his action. What I am suggesting is that theorists carry their human nature into their science, and this is shown by their willingness to explain puzzling events in motivational terms. They make a concerted effort to establish what the actors are "trying" to do. Once this is "discovered," then the theorist feels as if he "understands" what is taking place. Imputing to organizations and their members the disposition toward "rationality" reduces the unease of theorists, but in reality it says very little about the members themselves.

THE CONSEQUENCES OF ORGANIZING: SIMMEL'S VIEW

So far, several prominent concepts in organization theory have been introduced and illustrated by means of their correspondence with events portrayed in "Majority Rule." The major emphasis has been on the process of organizing, distinctions that emerge during its occurrence, and pressures toward dissolution that are implicit in the process. At various points in the discussion reference has been made to stable residues of the organizing process (e.g., tall versus flat organizations). While the earlier emphasis was on ways in which properties emerge, we now wish to broaden the discussion to include several regularities that one should be able to observe if he watches groups. We are intentionally shifting from concepts that are largely organizational to those that characterize groups in general. This shift is consistent with the earlier argument that organizations and groups are more similar than different.

The following discussion is based on Georg Simmel's essay written in 1917, entitled "The Social and Individual Level" (see 1950 translation, pp. 26-39). This particular essay was chosen because it is provocative though not well known, and, more importantly, because it contains the core of many ideas that have been amplified and made more prominent in later empirical studies of groups. It should be made clear that even though Simmel's distinctions are between individual and group action, they are *not* to be read as demonstrating the existence of a "group mind" (Asch, 1952, pp. 242-259). When Simmel discusses properties of groups, he is saying that the actions of individuals in the group become orderly because they interlock with and take account of the actions of other individuals. It is precisely because social behaviors are contingent on the actions of others that they are at the same time coherent and distinctive.

Groups Vacillate Less Than Individuals

Simmel argues that group actions are typically more direct, less ambivalent, less hesitant, and less confused than are the actions of individuals. He argues that a group "always knows whom to consider its enemy and whom its friend. Furthermore, it shows less discrepancy than the individual between will and deed, and between means and ends" (1950, p. 27). Presumably, this directness of action occurs because people share egoistic aims and associate in order to attain them. An individual's aims may include "insurance of his existence, the acquisition of new property, the pleasure derived from the maintenance and expansion of his power, and the protection of his possessions" (p. 27).

Contemporary research on groups provides some evidence that groups do vacillate less than individuals. A recurrent finding is that groups seldom plan, even when given the opportunity to do so (e.g., Cohen, Bennis, and

Wolkon, 1962; Hoffman, 1965; Shure *et al.*, 1962). It has repeatedly been found that when groups are assigned a task, they immediately start to perform it and spend little time considering alternative performance strategies. Furthermore, in discussion groups, members tend to evaluate immediately any solution that is offered. As soon as a solution is presented (even if it is incomplete), it is judged as good or bad and then used or discarded. The tendency of groups to evaluate solutions before they assemble all possibilities is one of the reasons why brainstorming (Osborn, 1953) has been recommended. When a group brainstorms, all suggestions are assembled before evaluation occurs. Apparently, only when evaluation is prohibited will groups consider a wide range of alternatives. If immediate evaluation is permitted, groups seem to settle for satisfactory solutions, to underexploit resources, and to balk when deliberation is urged.

Maier's (e.g., 1950, 1963) research on discussion groups is relevant to Simmel's argument because Maier states that the chief problem in discussion groups is that they are solution-minded rather than problem-minded (e.g., Maier and Solem, 1962). Groups look for solutions even before they are certain what the problem is. Since the main product of a problem-solving group is a solution, when such a group forms, its immediate action is to look for a solution. The fact that the resulting solution may be unsatisfactory seems to be of lesser importance. Activities that are not directly related to producing solutions (e.g., planning, discussion, generating alternatives, withholding evaluation) are not likely to occur unless substantial efforts are made to override the group's solution-mindedness (e.g., Maier and Hoffman, 1960).

It should be emphasized that one need not accept Simmel's explanation of shared egoistic aims to appreciate that nonvacillation exists. The crucial point is that when we compare group actions with those of individuals, we are likely to find that individuals are more intellective, more thoughtful, and less daring than are aggregates. This line of reasoning implies that investigators who have proposed that groups solve problems in much the same way as individuals (e.g., Bales, 1950) may be incorrect.

But there is an even more fascinating twist to the argument. Existing research does show that there are occasions when groups behave in just as contemplative a manner as do individuals (e.g., Maier and Hoffman, 1960). Simmel's argument implies that the greater directness of groups occurs when egoistic aspirations are shared and pursued. When the content of the discussion involves these aspirations, groups should be solution-minded. Much of Maier's research, for instance, involves discussion topics that directly affect the aspirations of individuals (e.g., how to set up a vacation schedule or handle job rotation). Thus it is not surprising that his groups tend to push for immediate solutions. But if we pursue Simmel's argument further, it is conceivable that individual and group modes of problem-solving would be more similar if they involved discussion of problems with nonegoistic ends.

This partially accounts for Bales' point of view mentioned above, since the groups that he observed often discussed topics that were less egoistic (see Bales and Strodtbeck, 1951, p. 490 for a list of topics discussed).

Groups Form Around Primitive Issues

The statement that groups form around egoistic issues is elaborated in the next portion of Simmel's essay. He argues that only "primitive forms," forms "that are inferior in terms of finesse and intellectuality," are the basis for association. He reasons that this is so "because it is the existence of these elements alone that we can be relatively sure of in *all* individuals" (p. 28). Stated in another way, "what is common to all can be the property of only those who possess least" (p. 37). Thus older capacities, those with a longer evolutionary history, are the ones that are most widely diffused and most available as bases for association. Recently acquired capacities are assumed to be more variable, more complex, and less widely distributed. While this reasoning may appear to be largely biological, Simmel intends it to be extended to nonheritable factors.

> There also are intellectual traits that manifest themselves in words and knowledge, in orientation of feeling, and in norms of will and judgment. As traditions, both conscious and unconscious, they permeate the individual; and the more so, the more generally, firmly, and unquestionably they have become parts of the intellectual life of his society—that is, the older they are. To the same extent, however, they are also less complex; they are coarser and closer to the immediate manifestations and necessities of life. As they become more refined and differentiated, they lose the probability of being the property of all. Rather they become more or less individual, and are only accidentally shared with others.[3]

Anecdotal support for the view that people coalesce around simple, absolute ideas is provided by Toch (1966) in his study of social movements. One of his conclusions is that movements form around extremely pessimistic or extremely optimistic views of the world. The important point is that movements form because views are *extreme*. They are not refined, subtle, or complicated. Instead, they consist of simple ideas invested with considerable affect.

The importance of primitive issues can also be seen in the phenomenon of "cultural lag" (Ogburn, 1922). It has been observed repeatedly that when groups undergo change, artifacts and peripheral contents are modified more rapidly than attitudes. This suggests that individuals originally coalesce

---

[3] From G. Simmel, *The Sociology of Georg Simmel*, trans. K. H. Wolff (New York: Free Press, 1950), pp. 28-29. Copyright © 1950 by The Macmillan Company. Reprinted by permission.

around shared attitudes (Newcomb, 1961). Having done so they retain these attitudes, even if they prove maladaptive, because they *are* shared and they provide a stable basis for reciprocal actions.

Simmel's argument is helpful only if one can establish which ideas have temporal priority and the greater probability of being widely diffused. Scott (1963) has provided one answer to this question. He has summarized considerable evidence which shows that affective distinctions (i.e., feelings of like and dislike) develop before the ability to make cognitive distinctions. Affect is the initial means an infant uses to order his world. Events are sorted initially into things that are pleasurable or painful, approached or avoided. These distinctions are made before any reasons for these preferences can be stated. Thus, shared affect could be a more salient basis for group formation than shared cognitions. Furthermore, if shared beliefs are tied to shared affect, then group formation should be even more likely.

There is the additional implication that if a group forms around complex beliefs that are relatively free of affect, the group will persist only if affect is generated or discovered. Earlier it was mentioned that groups are prone to evaluate solutions as soon as they are presented. This suggests that groups respond affectively to issues that are largely cognitive. If groups are unable to suspend judgment and if they respond with strong affect to suggestions that are made, then it could be argued that what these studies show is the emergence of a more basic ground for association. The group drifts toward a basic similarity, a preference for evaluation, and this preference, at least developmentally, precedes the tendency to analyze.

The Significance of Similarity and Dissimilarity

Undoubtedly, the most prominent assertion in group research is that people like and interact with those who are most similar to them (e.g., Festinger, 1954; Homans, 1961; Riecken and Homans, 1954; Lott and Lott, 1965; Newcomb, 1956). Unfortunately, investigators who adopt this proposition have been less articulate about dissimilarity, what its consequences are, what value it has, and how it is handled in groups. It is frequently proposed that there are pressures within groups toward uniformity, but nothing is said about pressures toward dissimilarity.

Simmel's view of similarity and dissimilarity is summarized in this statement: "Similarity, as fact or as tendency, is no less important than difference. In the most varied forms, both are the great principles of all external and internal development" (p. 30).

It is Simmel's description of dissimilarity that is of particular interest, since it provides a useful antidote to the current emphasis on similarity as the pervasive dynamic in groups.

> For the actions of the individual, his difference from others is of far greater interest than is his similarity with them. It largely is differentiation from others that challenges and determines our

> activity. We depend on the observation of their differences if we want to use them and adopt the right attitude toward them. Our practical interest concentrates on what gives us advantages and disadvantages in our dealings with them, not on that in which we coincide.[4]

The argument here is that individuals feel significant and unique largely when they are able to contrast themselves with others. Consequently, any explanation of social life must take into account the continuing efforts by participants to make themselves *both* more like and more unlike their associates. There will be a continuing tension between perceiving similarities in the interest of preserving group ties, and perceiving dissimilarities to establish individuality. Ambivalence, therefore, should be prominent in most groups.

Perhaps the best example of current theorizing which incorporates the dual pressures toward individualism and socialization as the main dynamic is Ziller's (1964) work. He summarized several research traditions in social psychology and concluded that all of them provide evidence that persons continually vacillate between uniting with and disbanding from their associates. Like Simmel, Ziller interprets this vacillation as a means of identity maintenance.

Groups Are Predominantly Emotional

The assertion that groups are predominantly emotional expands the point made earlier that affect precedes cognition in development. Simmel argues that group members are persuaded more by emotional than by intellectual appeals, because feelings are the primary means by which members are linked.

> If one arranges psychological manifestations in a genetic and systematic hierarchy, one will certainly place, at its basis, feeling (though naturally not *all* feelings), rather than intellect. Pleasure and pain, as well as certain instinctive feelings that serve the preservation of the individual and species, have developed prior to all operations with concepts, judgments and conclusions. Thus, the development of the intellect, more than anything else, reveals the lag of the social behind the individual level, whereas the realm of feeling may show the opposite.[5]

Simmel regards emotions as important for other reasons, besides the fact that they induce group formation. He puzzles over the fact that when people are together, there appears to be something like "collective excita-

---

[4]From Simmel, *op. cit.*, p. 30. Reprinted by permission.

[5]From Simmel, *op. cit.*, pp. 34-35. Reprinted by permission.

tion," "an excitation that cannot possibly be explained either in terms of him [the individual member] or of the matter at issue" (p. 35). While Simmel's language is imprecise, he could be referring to the phenomenon of social facilitation (Allport, 1924; Zajonc, 1965). Social facilitation theory argues that when persons are in groups, their level of arousal is heightened and they tend to emit with greater frequency, rapidity, and intensity those responses which they are disposed to emit in the situation. This theory complements Simmel's arguments. We would expect that when people associate, their most salient disposition (the response that is highest in the response hierarchy) would be to respond affectively. Simmel does not specify which feeling will occur, only that feeling as a general reaction will be uppermost.

CONCLUSION

The preceding discussion of Simmel has described some common elements that furnish a basis for association, and some ways in which these elements affect ongoing groups. By now, the observant reader is probably ready to take issue with the titles we have attached to the sections on the grook and on Simmel. The first title stated that the illustration was about organizing, yet much of the discussion was about processes that were already organized. The second title suggested that the section was about the consequences of organizing, yet many of the comments pertained to creating an organization rather than to its stable form. This dual emphasis on structure and process actually is unavoidable if one is to understand the working of an organization. An organization can be understood only in terms of the processes that are underway, or its organizing activities, yet it is possible to see regularities in these activities. Organizing and the consequences of organizing are actually inseparable—they are interchangeable notions. The same things are involved and we can call them either organizing or organization depending on how broad a portion of time we observe. Viewing the collectivity for longer periods of time will create the impression that organizing is underway; viewing it for shorter periods will suggest that *an* organization exists. We observe either an ongoing process that appears "frozen" and steady because it is glimpsed only briefly, or we observe that the process is continuously changing if we watch for a longer span of time. The point is that the crucial events to be explained are processes, their structuring, modification, and dissolving. It is not the tangible fixtures in an organization that are crucial. These merely provide the media through which the processes are expressed. Since these media are themselves fairly stable features of the organization, it is easy to miss the point that they are important only as they become incorporated into the processes involved in organizing. Their tangibility and visibility has little to do with their degree of importance for understanding what occurs. Their importance lies solely in the shape they will give to the processes that occur over and over in any collectivity involving any number of props and persons.

CHAPTER TWO

Problems in Contemporary Organization Theory

There are several concepts, assumptions, and practices in current organization theory that seem to stifle the expansion and testing of theories. These impediments must be recognized and removed if a robust theory of organizations is to result. The following sections discuss pitfalls that the reader would be wise to avoid.

ANECDOTAL EVIDENCE AS THE EMPIRICAL BASE

Any discipline will rise or fall depending on the reliability and validity of the observations on which its theories are based. Few fields have made so much of so little as has organization theory. The large number of theories, concepts, and prescriptions in this field far outdistances the empirical findings on which they are supposed to be grounded. For instance, considerable use has been made of anecdotal case studies. Even though case studies have a richness of detail, they have at least four drawbacks: they are (1) situation-specific, (2) ahistorical, (3) tacitly prescriptive, and (4) one-sided. These four items are drawbacks because of their effect on theory construction.

Any organizational environment is turbulent and contains several barriers to survival and growth of the individual. Organizations are demanding and not everyone can survive these demands, at least not without sizable cost. A goodly number of organizational case studies describe ways of "making out" or getting by in a basically alien environment (e.g., Bass, 1967b). They imply that if the reader took seriously the author's remarks, he could do a "better" job threading his way through the intricacies of the organization. The problem comes when we try to build theory from a case study. We can learn from it what to do and not do to survive in that particular environment, but we learn much less about the environment itself and why those particular adjustments are the best ones. Even if we get some idea of what it is in the environment that makes the author's remarks accurate, we still don't know what will happen if the environment changes and if the capacities of persons within the organization shift. This is what we mean when we say that case studies are situation-specific. In essence, we are forced into a more static view of the organization by the simple fact that mechanisms associated with processes, change, development, restructuring, and fluidity are not highlighted.

Now it is true that many case studies involve organizations undergoing stress or change (e.g., Barnes, 1960; Lawrence, 1958; O'Connell, 1968; Whyte and Hamilton, 1964). In fact, the bulk of case studies deal with circumstances where a problem exists and there is a great deal of unease among the members. These descriptions supply a vivid slice of life in organizations and depict what it feels like to be immersed in big trouble which must be handled by cumbersome organizational mechanisms. But this type of information isn't very helpful in theory construction. Theories are built on regularities among events, people, and relationships, not on sporadic, infrequent, explosive episodes. The point is that there are repetitive behaviors and events that constitute order in an organization whether they are reported in the case study or not. Getting into trouble can be just as orderly and repetitious as getting out. It is these regularities which theory attempts to capture, and it is precisely these regularities which are absent from many case studies. We are not arguing that repetition is more important than novelty or uniqueness. Instead, we are saying that the bulk of action is repetitive rather than nonrepetitive. The warrant for this assumption can be argued in terms of psychoanalytic theory (LaBarre, 1968), evolutionary theory (Campbell, 1965b), learning theory (Skinner, 1963), role theory (Kahn *et al.,* 1964), or cybernetic theory (MacKay, 1968). What we are saying here is that case studies are ahistorical. It is difficult to tell what the group being described has done in the past that is being *repeated* in the present, and it is even harder to discover what it is about the environment that produces this repetition. Precisely this information is needed if lawful relationships are to be stated.

The usefulness of a theory is *not* determined by its usability in the everyday business of running an organization or "making out" in one.

Theoretical usefulness is not defined in terms of pragmatics. Most case studies, however, are pragmatically based or can be read pragmatically. This means that a case study will tell us what works and what doesn't work in a particular organization. It will often provide a tacit "prescription" for getting along in the organization. But we do not know the conditions under which that pragmatic recommendation or prescription holds. Consider, for example, a case study that describes a set of circumstances in which a problem eventually was solved when members participated more fully in the decisions that affected them. This has a "lesson." The lesson is: if you want better decisions, let those who will be affected by them make them. We are tempted to state this in terms of a "law": as participation increases, the acceptability of a decision will increase. But a statement like this actually *hinders* theory construction. What we know is that participation affects decision acceptance. But we are left with the question: under what conditions? It is *not* a universal law that every time there is a change in participation, there is a corresponding change in decision acceptance. Sometimes yes, sometimes no. What we have to discover and build into a theory are precisely those elements that condition this relationship. That information is seldom available in a case study.

Most case studies do not describe any circumstances where the author's prescription *did not* work. They are one-sided; that is, the author does not provide us with a meaningful comparison so that we can see what it is that produces the regularity he sees. We can determine the causative factors only if we have a set of circumstances in which his observed regularity fails to occur. By comparing the circumstances at the time of failure with the circumstances at the time of success, we can determine what is common and what is different between the two. It is this information that enables us to construct a theory about organizations which will contain a realistic set of lawful relationships.

The inadequacy of organization theory's empirical base cannot be blamed solely on case studies. Field experiments on organizational problems also are culpable, as was demonstrated recently by Carey's (1967) extensive criticism of the most venerable set of field experiments in organization theory, the Hawthorne studies (Roethlisberger and Dickson, 1939). Carey makes it abundantly clear that these studies, which many theorists use as a point of departure, are replete with erroneous interpretations and do not demonstrate what everyone thought they did. For example, Carey refutes the conclusion, drawn from these studies, that relaxed and friendly supervision causes higher productivity. On closer inspection, the Hawthorne studies actually reveal the opposite relationship—because of higher productivity, the managers became more relaxed. Furthermore, the increase in productivity was caused by a simple change of personnel in the work group. Two recalcitrant workers were dismissed halfway through the study and were replaced by two women who needed jobs in order to handle their financial problems. Their efforts and prodding led to an increase in the group's output, and it was only *after* this output increase that the management relaxed the coercive style of supervision they had used previously. The fact that higher productivity causes managers to become more considerate has been recently demonstrated in the laboratory by Lowin and Craig (1968).

These findings are of great importance because so much organization theory and practice has assumed all along that the style of supervision affects productivity. The fact that the reverse direction of causation is just as likely demonstrates clearly the necessity for greater care and precision in experimentation and theory construction. Premature application of dubious findings is fatal both for practice and theory. Actually, it is not surprising that managers in business organizations are often disappointed by the results and recommendations produced by behavioral scientists. The problem is not that the theories are too abstract to be applied. Managers have sufficient intelligence to understand that a scientist's job is to develop theories that eventually may address practical issues *if* they are developed consistently and are tested with precision (e.g., Lundberg, 1968). The real problem is that current methods of theory construction and data collection drive a wedge between the world portrayed in the theories and the real world. The reinterpretation of the Hawthorne studies demonstrates this point. When these results were originally published, managers interested in improving output understandably latched onto them, as did organization theorists. But they did so without close scrutiny of what actually had been demonstrated.

The implications of this analysis should be clear. Reliable data are needed for generating and testing useful theories. The data have to be unambiguous, and the only way we can generate unambiguous data is by using techniques that resolve ambiguity. To accomplish this, we typically need multiple methods, or techniques which are imperfect in *different* ways. When multiple methods are applied, the imperfections in each method tend to cancel one another, and the resulting data are less ambiguous. As we have said over and over, the likelihood that clear data will be produced depends on the number and kinds of comparisons that are made. The experimental method, whether applied in field experiments (e.g., Scott, 1965; Seashore, 1966), controlled naturalistic observation (e.g., Weick, 1968), contrived laboratory experiments (e.g., Weick, 1965, 1967), or simulated environments (e.g., Abt Associates, 1965; Drabek and Haas, 1967; Guetzkow, 1962, 1968) is the principal tactic by which more durable and useful data can be obtained. The several variations that are possible within the experimental method permit the canceling of imperfections. There are techniques available that, if applied with sufficient concern for detail, can provide the data which case studies seldom do. And they can provide these data with more frequency than even the best case studies can. It is routine for an experimental method to produce useful data. It is exceptional when case studies do so.

CONSIDERING MANAGEMENT PROBLEMS
IN MANAGEMENT TERMS

Organization theory has often been stifled because it has worked on problems that managers thought were problems and has studied them using managerial concepts rather than psychological or sociological ones. The only way in which understanding can be advanced is if the symbols used by practitioners are removed, and the phenomena recast into language that has psychological or sociological meaning. For example, managers talk about line-staff relationships, span of control, the size of departments, cost-efficiency ratios, etc. This is managerial talk and it helps managers get on with their work of managing. But managerial talk carves up the world of the organization in a particular way. It isolates certain phenomena and certain implications. If a psychologist decides to develop empirical laws about "line-staff relationships" he already is at a disadvantage. He tacitly accepts the manager's definition of the problem *and* the relevant components. He takes the phenomenon that the manager points to and his way of pointing to it as the principal arena in which the search for relationships should be conducted. There is little chance that he can gain an understanding of the phenomenon psychologically, or build this understanding into a framework that will have broader relevance. All he can do is tack on selected psychological concepts to a problem with little psychological relevance. For example, a manager might observe that whenever his department contains more than 25 people, morale drops sharply. If a theorist takes this observation at face value, and then proceeds to develop a theory of the effects of size on morale, he is not likely to tell us anything of theoretical importance. The problem has been phrased in managerial, not psychological, terms. If instead of looking at gross changes in size, the investigator were to study the more basic psychological questions, such as what happens to people when they feel crowded, ignored, anonymous, on display, or unmonitored, then the chance of understanding the effects of size would improve. Linkages between size and morale would become more apparent because the psychologist would be exploring psychological states that mediate this effect; the resulting theory would be applicable to a wider variety of settings than those in which the manager operates (e.g., the psychologist could predict what would happen in husband-wife dyads when the husband felt crowded); and the psychologist would be in a better position to link his theory with other theories and move toward unification of knowledge (e.g., the theory might suggest that crowding is an instance of the more general phenomenon of approach-avoidance gradients; Schneirla, 1959). Note that all of these latter benefits can be realized only if the scientist remains faithful to and exploits his discipline's strengths. After all, he is equipped to do what the average layman cannot, namely, to conduct psychological or sociological analyses of everyday phenomena. He abandons most of his tools for doing such analyses if he accepts managerial problems phrased in managerial terms.

An interesting paradox arises. Most scientists want the knowledge they have obtained to be accepted by other people, to make a difference in their lives, and to improve the human condition in some way. They have every right to want this, because they may know something with greater certainty than anyone else does. But generating something acceptable and true is possible only if the scientist first *ignores* the everyday labels with which the phenomenon comes to him, and replaces these labels with symbols he can work with. Only if he does this can he discover truths that deserve acceptance. If the scientist is concerned with acceptability from the start, then the chance that he will produce anything acceptable in the long run is reduced. You have to destroy acceptability in order to produce it.

There is a growing awareness that working within the constraints of managerial language is a severe deterrent to understanding. Pugh makes the following assertion about industrial psychology:

> Their [those in the field of industrial psychology] overwhelming limitation is that almost without exception, they have defined their work in terms of management problems, not psychological ones, and this has turned them from scientists into applied scientists or technologists. ... It is no criticism to be an applied scientist if there is some science to apply. But applied psychology is a contradiction in terms because there is yet no coherent body of acceptable theory and data which can be drawn upon and applied once we get beyond the level of learning of perceptual and motor skills.[1]

This same argument can also be found in Merton (1963), Krech's excerpt from a talk by Titchener (1968), and Heiskanen (1967).

SIZE AS A CONFOUNDED VARIABLE

Size, whether defined in terms of number of machines, people, relationships, or total output, is an obvious distinguishing property of collectivities, and numerous investigators have given it prominence in their theoretical formulations (e.g., Indik, 1963). However, in spite of the clear variation in size from collectivity to collectivity, it is not apparent that size is a meaningful point of departure to gain an understanding of organizations. In the literature on groups there is a running debate over questions such as "how many is small?", "when does small become large?", and "what is the crucial

---

[1]From D. S. Pugh, "Modern Organization Theory," *Psychological Bulletin, 66* (1966), p. 243. Reprinted by permission.

dividing point, in terms of number of people, at which group processes undergo a radical transformation?" Concern with "smallness" has prevailed at the expense of other potentially more useful dimensions. For example, a common assertion in literature about groups (e.g., Lorge *et al.*, 1958) is that most researchers study *ad hoc,* short-lived, temporary groups and that these groups behave differently from groups of longer duration. Duration of contact may be a more crucial determinant of group behavior than number of people (e.g., Hall and Williams, 1966; Gartner and Iverson, 1967).

Our point is not that size is irrelevant. There are many ways in which it has been shown to have distinct effects. But size, *per se,* is a misleading variable if it is used as the starting point of an inquiry. Whenever there is a change in size, *several* things happen. This means that when groups of differing size are compared, one never knows how to interpret the comparison. For example, in a 12-man group, as compared to a three-man group, (1) it is more difficult to communicate to everyone, (2) there is not sufficient time for everyone to talk, (3) there is more need for a leader and greater likelihood that he will control what happens, (4) members are more likely to form into smaller clusters to maintain intimate contact, (5) differences in participation rates become exaggerated, etc. Given these differences, what are we to conclude when a scientist says that a group of three is more productive than a group of 12? Conceivably, any one of the five differences by itself *or* some complex interaction between two or more of these five, could produce the outcome.

The number of persons in a group may at times be crucial, but this is true mostly of very small numbers. The crucial transitions are those from one person to two, from two to three, from three to four, from four to seven, and from seven to nine. The justification for the importance of these transitions can be stated succinctly. The transition from one to two creates the basic unit of social behavior, the dyad. In a dyad there is interdependence, reciprocal behavior, and the necessity for accommodation to another person. The transition from two to three is significant because now there exists the possibility of an alliance between two members against the third one. The phenomena of control, cooperation *and* competition, and influence are produced by this transition. A triad also is less vulnerable than a dyad. If one person leaves, a social unit still remains. But if one person leaves a dyad, the social unit dissolves. The transition from three to four creates the possibility of two equal dyads or alliances, and this may perpetuate both the social unit and the problems of control. The significant feature of four is that an alliance between two members is not sufficient to gain control. The excluded pair may themselves form an alliance, in which case the possibility of a stalemate increases. The jump from four to seven is crucial because just as individuals can form coalitions in the interest of control, so can groups. A seven-man group has the potential of splitting into two dyads and a triad. If the two dyads combine resources, they can gain some control over the larger triad. But if the triad can keep the dyads apart or can persuade one of the dyads to join it, then the triad will be in control. Perfect symmetry with regard to all the processes we have described would be found in the nine-man group. Here there can exist three groups of three. This permits coalitions *within* a specified triad and coalitions *between* a pair of triads. This property of coalitions within and between is not possible in the case of seven.

These basic control and authority relationships are the essential ones in large as well as small groups. If we can understand how nine people go about the work of getting organized, producing, dissolving, and restructuring, then we shouldn't find that many surprises when we watch 1000 people go through the same activities. Size is important largely in terms of the problems of control and affiliation that it raises and the alternative solutions that it provides for solving these problems. Most of these problems are evident in rather small units. In laboratory studies, then, the scientist is free to use small groups, in which he can observe with greater clarity just what is happening. It is important to understand that this is not an argument in which we have subtly transformed a vice into a virtue, as is often charged (e.g., Mills, 1967, pp. 42-56). The argument that two, three, four, seven, and nine persons are crucial units is not meant to justify the typical laboratory studies of groups that contain only these numbers. Instead, the argument is based on processes, and on the fact that different processes are triggered when different combinations of people are possible. The basic combinations necessary to trigger the relevant processes are contained within the transitions we have mentioned.

WHAT IS "ORGANIZATIONAL BEHAVIOR"?

The literature about organizations is laden with a troublesome phrase: "organizational behavior." The phrase "organizational behavior" is troublesome because one is never certain whether it means behavior that occurs within some specified place, behavior with reference to some place, behavior controlled by an organization, behavior that constitutes an organization, or just what. The trouble deepens if we inquire further. Behavior is behavior, isn't it? What is gained by introducing the qualifier "organizational"? If we search for instances of organizational behavior, we may be tempted to look for unique behaviors that occur when people act within organizational roles. The problem with this type of search should be obvious. Events inside organizations resemble events outside; sensitivities of the worker inside are continuous with sensitivities outside. Since people have as much desire to integrate the various portions of their life as to compartmentalize them, what happens inside affects what happens outside, and vice versa. This is a roundabout way of saying that continuity from setting to setting is more likely than discontinuity. In that sense, behavior is behavior, and though its form may be shaped by the particular setting in which it unfolds, it still unfolds with a certain degree of orderliness, regularity, and predictability. Rather than searching for unique behaviors that occur within an organization and then building a theory about this uniqueness, it seems more useful to build theories about the particular ways that enduring individual dispositions are *expressed* in an organizational setting, and about the effects of this expression. If we take seriously the growing number of statements that the differences between work and play are getting smaller and smaller (e.g., Lewis and Brisset, 1967; Mead, 1963; Riesman, Potter, and Watson, 1960), then the argument for studying behavior rather than organizational behavior becomes even more apparent. Organizations may pose unique problems for their members and furnish unique mechanisms by which these problems are handled, but it is still people who implement these mechanisms, and the behaviors are the same as the behaviors that implement family, recreational, or community mechanisms (e.g., Bradney, 1957).

The argument that organizational behavior is continuous with behavior in other settings can be made from a different perspective. There are several investigators who make the convincing argument that responses or actions can be viewed as sequences of component acts which run off intact once they are triggered (e.g., Mandler, 1964; Roby, 1966). This assumption can be coupled with the further one that people select or notice those stimuli that enable response sequences to be run off. George Herbert Mead (1956) states this latter assumption: "An act is an impulse that maintains the life process by the selection of certain sorts of stimuli it needs. Thus, the organism creates its environment. The stimulus is the occasion for the expression of the impulse. Stimuli are means, tendency is the real thing. Intelligence is the selection of stimuli that will set free and maintain life and aid in rebuilding it" (p. 120). To rephrase Mead's point, man notices those stimuli which permit him to do what he wants to do. What he wants to do is to continue living, to protect the "essential states" (Ashby, 1956) that enable living to continue. Living consists of expressing dispositions, tendencies, responses. Thus behavior can be viewed as responses in search of appropriate stimuli or "excuses" for expression. Though an organization may contain stimuli unlike those encountered in nonorganizational settings, these stimuli remain only potential stimuli until they are noticed. And Mead's point is that response repertoires control noticing. The person carries this repertoire and its implications for noticing wherever he goes. Thus, if one gains an understanding of response repertoires, and the conditions under which attention is controlled by the content of these repertoires, then a more substantial theory about organizations and behaviors can be built. The theory would concentrate on attention rather than on action. It would essentially ask the question, "How are the processes and contents of attention influenced by the conditions of task-based interdependency found in those collectivities which we conventionally designate as organizations?" Rendered in this form the question is complex, but it is also much more specific than the question,

"What is organizational behavior and how is it influenced?" Defining organizational behavior in terms of processes of attention directs the investigator toward specific processes and properties within an organization that he might ordinarily have overlooked. He is sensitized to a specific set of events and behaviors in a way that is impossible given a more general definition of organizational behavior.

Thus the term "organizational behavior" serves no useful guiding function. It generates questions mostly about what it means. It misleads the investigator by implying that he should search for differences rather than common characteristics. It also tempts him to exaggerate the importance of those differences that he does find, thus increasing the danger that he will end up with concepts which cannot be related to anything else. The term "organizational behavior" neither sensitizes the investigator to anything crucial nor translates into any specific questions.

WHAT IS THE "ENVIRONMENT"?

Whenever we tackle a phenomenon so apparently large and complex as a human organization, we inevitably run into boundary problems. If we try to talk about an organization's adaptation to its environment, the following questions arise: What is "included" within the organization, and available for purposes of adapting? What is "outside," or "excluded" from the organization, that must be adapted to? Failure to handle boundary issues has beset a large number of organization theories and has made understanding and unification more difficult. One man's internal system turns out to be another man's external system. For instance, there has been a running debate on the question, "Are customers members of the organization, or are they part of the environment to which the organization must adapt?" (See Barnard, 1948, pp. 118-125.)

Not yet taken seriously by organization theorists is the possibility suggested in the quotation from Mead mentioned earlier (see p. 26). The predominant model of man adopted by organization theorists is one in which the human is essentially reactive to the environmental contingencies that occur. This environment can be inside or outside the organization, but in either case the actor essentially reacts to it as given. However, instead of adapting to a ready-made environment, it is entirely possible that the actors *themselves* create the environment to which they adapt (Asch, 1952, p. 256). Rather than talking about adapting to an external environment, it may be more correct to argue that organizing consists of adapting to an enacted environment, an environment which is *constituted by* the actions of interdependent human actors.

Several theories do contain the assumption that members of organizations often try to reshape the environment in ways that permit the organization to make better use of its resources (e.g., Katz and Kahn, 1966). These theories say that organizations attempt to act in a proactive rather than reactive manner, but typically are only moderately effective in doing so. The organizations create some changes in the environment, but in general they still must adapt to contingencies over which they have no control. A stronger form of this assertion would be that organizations are *always* proactive. They create and constitute the environment to which they react; the environment is put there by the actors within the organization and by no one else. This reasserts the argument that the environment is a phenomenon tied to processes of attention, and that unless something is attended to it doesn't exist. While this is a rather radical turnabout in the way environments are usually discussed, there is precedent for this view in organization theory itself (e.g., Pugh, 1966; March and Simon, 1958), in empirical research (e.g., Stager, 1967; Tuckman, 1964, 1967), and in theories of how people discover knowledge (e.g., Merleau-Ponty, 1963; Schutz, 1967).

A more detailed statement of the argument for an enacted environment will be presented later (see p. 63 ff.). Our point here is that existing organization theories are inexplicit about what constitutes the environment. Many organization theories argue that organizations can be understood as contrived mechanisms for adapting to environmental contingencies in the pursuit of goals. The trouble with this argument is that one can never be certain just what is adapting to what. To say that the organization adapts to itself and to that which is not itself, doesn't say much. We need to know specifically what is being adapted to by what means. Until adaptation is localized and boundaries between inside and outside are removed or made more explicit, it will be difficult to know very much about what an organization is, what it does, or why it does it.

As a final comment regarding the issue of environments, it should be noted that one of the more promising ways of treating the environment is in terms of information. Rather than regarding the crucial environment of organizations as consisting of raw materials and consumers of transformed raw materials, it seems possible to gain a more complete view of what happens if we take information and meaning as the critical commodities on which organizations operate, to which their processes are directed, and in terms of which their relations are established. Katz and Kahn describe this outlook:

> [C]ommunication, the exchange of information and the transmission of meaning, is the very essence of a social system or an organization. The input of physical energy is dependent on information about it, and the input of human energy is made possible through communicative acts. Similarly the transformation of energy (the accomplishment of work) depends upon communication between people in each organizational subsystem and upon communication

between subsystems. The product exported carries meaning as it meets needs and wants, and its use is further influenced by the advertising or public relations material about it.[2]

If the relevant environment for the organization is described in terms of information, then it is possible to argue that organizing is directed toward resolving the equivocality that exists in informational inputs judged to be relevant. Such an interpretation is consistent with the basic concept in information theory (e.g., Rapoport, 1953; Schramm, 1955; Weaver, 1949) that information results when uncertainty is removed. Any item of information contains several possibilities or implications. It is more or less ambiguous and is subject to a variety of interpretations. If action is to be taken, the possibilities must be narrowed and the equivocal properties of the message made more unequivocal. Organizing is concerned with removing equivocality from information and structuring processes so that this removal is possible.

RATIONALITY SANS BEHAVIOR

Even though most organizations are interested in productivity, and most organization theorists discuss determinants of productivity, existing theories of organizational behavior run into the same stubborn problem that has beset psychologists for some time: how does thought get translated into action? Although there have been several attempts to handle this problem (e.g., Campbell, 1963; Katz and Stotland, 1959; Miller, Galanter, and Pribram, 1960; Rokeach, 1966; Weick, 1966), these suggestions seem to have had little impact on organization theory. The assumption seems to be that once the perceptions of organizational members are affected, action consistent with these perceptions will follow automatically.

Part of the reason that linkages between beliefs and behavior have been underdeveloped is that behaviors that occur within the organization have been inadequately described (Dubin, 1962). Furthermore, there has not been sufficient appreciation of the fact that analysis of tasks performed and of the persons paired with the tasks is crucial to an understanding of organizational functioning (Miller and Hamblin, 1963; Morris, 1966; Pepinsky, Weick, and Riner, 1965; Perrow, 1967). Part of the reason that task analysis has been slighted is that there have not been a sufficient number of taxonomies for describing tasks, an inadequacy which shows some signs of being remedied (e.g., Altman, 1966; Hackman, in press). But even if tasks are

---

[2]From D. Katz and R. L. Kahn, *The Social Psychology of Organizations* (New York: Wiley, 1966), pp. 223-224. Reprinted by permission.

specified, and statements are made about the conditions under which tasks are accepted, there still remains the problem of specifying the precise ways in which acceptance is translated into a given amount of effort and into accomplishment of the task.

One reason why efforts to describe the linkage between belief and action have floundered is implied in an earlier discussion. It may be that cognition has little effect on behavior, because it follows rather than precedes behavior. Cognitions may be retrospective; they may make sense of what has happened rather than what will happen. Plans for the future may have little control over behavior, because they are basically content-free. It is actions that provide the content for cognitions, and in the absence of action, cognitions are vacuous.

The principal argument here is that too little attention has been paid to actions and too much to cognitions, plans, and beliefs. Cognitions may well summarize previous actions rather than determine future actions, yet this possibility has not been considered seriously.

PARTIAL INCLUSION

Theorists differ in their opinions regarding what portion of an organization's members is engaged in performing organizational activities. Several (e.g., Allport, 1955, 1962; Katz and Kahn, 1966; Steiner, 1955; Tannenbaum, 1968) argue that only selected behaviors of individuals are necessary for organizational functioning and it is these specific behaviors that are interlocked with those of other members. While it is true that whole persons rather than parts are hired, it is not true that all member behaviors are of equal importance. Other investigators, while acknowledging the fact of partial inclusion, discuss its implications for morale, satisfaction, productivity, and growth of the person involved (e.g., McGregor, 1960). Essentially, their argument is that if more of the person were engaged by the organization, then satisfaction and productivity would increase.

In their eagerness to "moralize" about the dysfunctions of partial inclusion, investigators have overlooked some of its dynamics. Earlier, it was noted that people retain dual interests in individuation and socialization. They wish to have both social ties and independence. Given these dual interests, it follows that partial inclusion provides conditions under which dual interests can be realized. Some of the person's behaviors are interlocked with those of other people, others are not. The organizational member is simultaneously individual and socialized. Furthermore, interlocked behaviors and the collective structure which they produce are commonly protected by the individual, so that the rewards that result from this interlocking are assured and are produced with regularity. People take steps, once a collective structure forms, to insure that it is preserved. This means that when there is partial inclusion or interlocking of some behaviors, additional behaviors of the individual may come under the control of this collective structure, because of his desire to stabilize it. It is the production of these structural assurances (Allport, 1962) which suggests that the actor may take responsibility for integrating more of himself into the organization. He does so by binding additional behaviors to the organization in order that collective structures may be maintained.

If one takes seriously the possibility that meaning is retrospective, then part of the debate regarding partial inclusion dissolves. If a person interlocks some of his behaviors with someone else's, and if these interlocked behaviors are protected by structural assurances, then it is possible that this subset of behaviors will become meaningful and attain closure when viewed retrospectively. An actor's "organizational life" consists of the things that he does at the organization and that he reconstructs into a meaningful life. While it may appear to an outside observer that the actor's capacities are not being used to the fullest, this may not be his circumstance at all. The meaning of the organization and of the actor's participation in it are defined solely in terms of what he does there. It is the actions that control his definition of what organizational behavior is.

There is the further point that behaviors not interlocked in the direct pursuit of organizational requirements might be interlocked informally with those of other workers. Most theorists acknowledge this possibility. The point being made can be summarized in terms of the argument that only parts of members are wanted and that members must "realize" this and act accordingly (e.g., Katz and Kahn, 1966). Our point is that the actor, unaided, tends to put closure around the actions he performs no matter how extensive or limited his involvement. It is unnecessary that he "realize" the fact of partial inclusion. He really can't do otherwise. It is true that he may retain desires or ambitions which are thwarted in his present job. But these exist apart from partial inclusion. He does not have the desires and ambitions because only part of his talents are being used. He simply has partial inclusion and desires.

OBSERVABLES AND PSYCHOLOGICAL EXPLANATIONS

There are several places in the organizational literature where investigators seem to resist defining their concepts in terms of observable actions by individuals in the mistaken belief that, in doing so, they will have to explain the actions psychologically. This belief is incorrect and has generated needless debate over the issue of how groups differ from individuals. The exact nature of the problem is described by Brodbeck:

> It is therefore misleading to say that because group concepts must be defined in terms of individuals they are "really" psychological.

Only if "psychological" is broadly defined to include all human behavior is this the case. In this sense, "selling short on the stock market" is psychological. But then the term is so broad as to be virtually useless. Only if this behavior can be explained with the context of a theory in psychology is it significantly called psychological rather than, say, economic.[3]

Thus, a commitment to study group behavior defined in terms of individual behaviors *is not* also a commitment to translate sociology into psychology. The basic questions in group research are: What happens when certain individuals are put together to perform a task? How do we describe the action that takes place? How do we predict what will happen? The field of psychology has no monopoly on answers to these questions. The economist, political scientist, philosopher, sociologist, and anthropologist all have valid explanations of behavior. However, all these explanations are worthless if they do not originate from an explicit set of observations that can be repeated by someone else.

To be more explicit, there is general agreement that defined properties of groups exist. People in aggregates behave differently than do people in isolation. Furthermore, there is agreement that all terms which are used to describe a group should refer to observables. Unless a concept refers to something that can be observed, one can never know whether a property is present or absent and in what amount. The only way to understand anything is to watch it, and this means we have to know what "it" is. Thus it is crucial that the terms used to describe a group refer to observables.

An individual and his actions *are* observable. Thus, if group properties can be defined in terms of observable individual behaviors, there is a better chance that empirical research on groups can be made cumulative. As we have said, scientists have sometimes been unwilling to define group behavior in terms of observable acts by individuals in the mistaken belief that they would also be forced to provide psychological explanations of these behaviors. But once a concept is anchored in something that other people can observe for themselves, the investigator is free to construct whatever explanation he wants. First, he has to establish a consensual starting point, a point that others can duplicate. Once this starting point is established, then anyone who looks at the same set of observations can build an explanation. While this may sound elementary, a surprising amount of confusion has occurred in group research because investigators have not understood the necessity of using observable individual behaviors.

Some theorists think that it is impossible, on scientific grounds, to reduce group actions to individual behaviors.

---

[3]From May Brodbeck, "Methodological Individualisms: Definition and Reduction," *Philosophy of Science, 25* (1958), p. 16. Copyright © 1958 by The Williams and Wilkins Co., Baltimore, Md. Reprinted by permission.

[A]re there attributes of groups not definable in terms of either the behavior of the individuals composing the group or the relations between these individuals or both? ... Can we speak, for example, of a "responsive audience" without defining the adjective in terms of the behavior of the individual people in the audience and some more or less precise statistical notion, namely, the percentage of attentive individuals in the group?[4]

Until recently, a surprisingly large number of individual behaviors have been ignored as potential components of group theory. If a scientist looks only at one or two gross bodily movements, then it is possible that he will not find any individual behaviors that exemplify group concepts. But this does not mean that observable individual behaviors cannot be used to define group concepts. The real problem is that the scientist is observing the "wrong" behaviors.

Given the arguments that group concepts must refer to observables, and that the most obvious source of observables in groups is the actions of individuals, these arguments must be leavened with reality. Defining group behavior in terms of individual actions is just an ideal to be approximated; there is at present no possibility for anything beyond approximation. This is so for the simple reason that observation of individuals is itself a fallible process done with fallible instruments.

An important caution must also be introduced. Even though we have used the phrase "observable individual behaviors," this should not be read as the "observable behavior of a single person." Given that interdependence is the crucial element from which a theory of organizations is built, *interacts* rather than acts are the crucial observables that must be specified. The unit of analysis is contingent response patterns, patterns in which an action by actor A evokes a specific response in actor B which is then responded to by actor A. This is the pattern designated a "double interact" by Barker and Wright (1955), and it is proposed by Hollander and Willis (1967) as the basic unit for describing interpersonal influence. Since organizing involves control, influence, and authority, a description of organizing must use the double interact as the unit of analysis for specifying observable behaviors. To see why this is so, suppose that a supervisor wants to get a worker to stop doing task A and start doing task B. The worker's action is the doing of task A; the supervisor tries to influence him to do task B. Obviously, we must know how the worker responds to this directive before we can make any statement about the effectiveness or ineffectiveness of the influence attempt. But to determine the worker's response, we need a specific description of his original activity, as a basis for comparison. The worker's typical response pattern will probably be altered in some way by the supervisor's directive, and before we can understand the meaning of this alteration, we

---

[4]From Brodbeck, *op. cit.*, p. 2. Reprinted by permission.

need to know the action that was already underway. This is the point in Atkinson and Cartwright's (1964) important argument that many existing theories of motivation are inadequate because they fail to take account of ongoing activity and the forces sustaining it when a substitute activity is proposed.

THE PROBLEM OF INERTIA

A large number of organization theories could legitimately be relabeled "theories of crisis." This is so because many of them have more to say about the pathology of organizations than about their normalcy. Nobody seems to know much about how organizations operate in untroubled times; the day-to-day, routine existence of organizations is not given much attention. In the world of the theories, organizations seem to lope along from crisis to crisis, and to do nothing very interesting in between.

This emphasis on pathology is misleading if it implies that routine activity is not problematic. Inertia and routine, ongoing affairs are not nearly as easy to explain as they might appear to be. This point is illustrated in Campbell's discussion of the importance of ecological pressure for the maintenance of complex structures which have been produced by processes of evolution.

> In general, complex structures such as the vertebrate eye are only maintained by consistent ecological pressure. Without this, the cumulative occurrence of unelimated mutations gradually destroys its functionality, and, combined with internal selection pressures in favor of simplicity, gradually removes its complexity. The more complex the structure the more statistically likely it becomes that random mutations will lessen rather than increase the adaptive adequacy. Or to revert to the learning model, the more the rat has learned of the maze, the more a random change in an element of his running pattern is likely to lead to increased error rather than to improvement. ... [T]his argument implies that where a complex structure seemingly persists, it is being sustained by ecological pressure even where the scientist does not yet understand what this pressure is. ... It opposes a parsimonious general law of cultural inertia. Instead, the inertia becomes something to be explained.[5]

[handwritten margin note: assumes pressures to simplicity in life.]

---

[5]From D. T. Campbell, "Variation and Selective Retention in Socio-cultural Evolution." In H. R. Barringer, G. I. Blanksten, and R. Mack (Eds.), *Social Change in Developing Areas* (Cambridge, Mass.: Schenkman, 1965). Quote is reprinted by permission from pp. 40-41.

If this argument is taken seriously, we can legitimately wonder how it is that any organization ever persists or continues to function given the complexity of relationships which it contains. And it is precisely this question which most organization theorists seldom ask or try to answer. The fact that an organization persists is remarkable, because there are persistent forces that can simplify and destroy the level of complexity that has been evolved. Routine acts, acts that are taken for granted, are extremely vulnerable to disruption (Garfinkel, 1963). Thus the statement that organizations are ongoing, an apparently innocuous assertion, in fact contains some of the most fascinating problems in organization theory.

CHAPTER THREE

Components of a Revised
Concept of Organization

In the preceding chapter several reservations about existing organization theory were expressed. These reservations imply something about the changes that should be made in a revised theory of organizations. These desirable changes are summarized below and are discussed in greater detail in subsequent chapters.

1. *Processes involved in organizing must continually be reaccomplished.* At any moment in time, there are possibilities inherent in the information on which an organization operates which, if noticed and actualized, can undermine the workings of the organization. There are always mutations which affect the workings of the organizational processes. These mutations occur continuously. Any process is always being diverted, modified, undone, simplified, or made less orderly. It is never true that a process simply unfolds time after time. Instead, in order for the process to unfold at any moment in time, its components must be reinstated, reaffirmed, and reaccomplished. Failure to do so can produce an irreversible change in the way the process unfolds. This irreversible modification may be detrimental, or it may be beneficial. For the moment this is unimportant. All we wish to stress is that processes are repetitive only if this repetitiveness is continuously accomplished. To make processes repetitive is problematic rather than routine. Since organizational processes never unfold in exactly the same way twice, they can only approximate an earlier mode of functioning, and this approximation is better or worse depending on the degree to which muta-

tions are discarded. It is for the reasons mentioned here that inertia is viewed as problematic. An intricate set of relationships is necessary to make inertia possible, and these relationships are easily disrupted.

2. *Control is a prominent process within organizations, but it is accomplished by relationships, not by people.* It is relationships and not people that impose control in an organization. This was evident in the discussion of the power retained by lower members in the situation of "Majority Rule." What was crucial was the relationships in which lower participants had the power to comply with or refuse orders given by higher participants. This is the reason why conditionality (Ashby, 1962) is such an important concept in organization theory. Conditionality means that the form and degree of the relationship between two components are conditioned by the state of a third component. Stated in another way, the pattern of conditionalities constitutes the control in any system. Control of the ways in which processes unfold and their consequences for other processes is determined by the specific, mutually causal relationships that are present in the system. People are the medium through which these relationships are made actual. But in the end it is the relationships, not the people, that constitute the control network.

3. *Goal consensus is not a precondition of order and regularity.* The common assertion that people organize in order to accomplish some agreed-upon end is not essential to an explanation of the orderliness found in concerted action, nor is goal-governed behavior that evident in organizations. Goals are sufficiently diverse, the future is sufficiently uncertain, and the actions on which goal statements could center are sufficiently unclear, that goal statements exert little control over action. Visible features such as profit, wages, productivity, and share of the market can be treated as the reasons for an organization's existence, but this begs such questions as why these particular goals were formulated, how widely they are diffused, and with what intensity they are held. The view common to most organization theories attributes to goals more stability than they seemingly have. It is probable that goals are tied more closely to actual activities than has been realized, and that they are better understood as summaries of *previous* actions. Much of the organization's work does not seem to be directed toward goal attainment. Instead, it can be understood more readily as actions with a primitive orderliness, this orderliness being enhanced retrospectively when members review what has come to pass as a result of the actions.

Two points made in the preceding discussions can now be placed in context. First, it was noted that persons retain competing tendencies to demonstrate similarity to and dissimilarity from their associates (see p. 15). The retention of these dual aims suggests that diverse goals will always be present in any group, and that these goals are basically incompatible. Individuation implies responses of disengagement and independence; socialization implies responses of engagement and dependence or interdependence. Ambivalence is a major feature of organized life, and to say that organized life is controlled by *shared* goals is to present an overly simplified picture.

The second point concerns the concept of "rationality" (see pp. 9-10). In the terminology of cognitive dissonance theory (e.g., Brehm and Cohen, 1962; Festinger, 1957) rationality seems better understood as a postdecision rather than a predecision occurrence. Rationality makes sense of what has been, not what will be. It is a process of justification in which past deeds are made to appear sensible to the actor himself and to those other persons to whom he feels accountable. It is difficult for a person to be rational if he does not know precisely what it is that he must be rational about. He can create rationality only when he has available some set of actions which can be viewed in several ways. It is possible for actors to make elaborate, detailed statements of their plans. However, the error comes if we assume that these plans then control their behavior. If we watch closely, it will become clear that the behavior is under the control of more determinants than just the vocally stated plan. And at the conclusion of the actions, it will never be true that the plan as first stated will have been exactly accomplished. But something will have been accomplished, and it is this something, and the making sense of this something, that constitute rationality. The mere statement that members are pursuing shared goals leaves too many questions unanswered.

4. *Triads are the basic unit of analysis in organization theory.* Three is the crucial number in organization theory. Three can pertain to people, or it can refer to two persons plus one object or one person plus two objects. The reason three is central is that it is the basic unit needed to demonstrate conditionality, a basic concept of organization theory. Organization is a mediated causal relationship between two items, in which the relationship between the two items is influenced by the state of a third item.

Although we are most concerned with multiperson situations, and the conditional ties among the processes that these persons activate, our argument does imply that a single person who coorients to two items of information is demonstrating a type of organizing.

5. *Attentional processes are a crucial determinant of human organizing.* Although several organization theories accord central importance to processes of perception, most of them do so in terms of enduring sets. Members "see" what they are attuned to see (e.g., Costello and Zalkind, 1963), and these perceptual sets are regarded as stable characteristics constituted on the basis of past experience. The perceptual sets are "ready-made" explanations that the actor carries from situation to situation.

Reliance on the concept of sets to explain behavior leaves too many problems unsolved. The concept of sets imputes a reactive quality to perception and misses the point that perception *creates* as well as reacts to an environment. The notion that sets are relatively enduring obscures the point that perception is influenced by pragmatics, by the particular here and now in which it originates. Perception is a more complex and general phenomenon than is attention. Thus a study of attention would appear to be a more logical and manageable starting point for an inquiry into the ways in which organizational environments are created. When we study attention, it is not important to discover immediately all prior experiences that an actor has had. Instead, the immediate question concerns what is happening in the actor's *present* situation that controls the nature of the attention he directs to his past experience.

6. *Organizations continue to exist only to the degree that they are able to maintain a balance between flexibility and stability.* Even though this sounds like an innocuous assertion, it actually points out one of the more crucial requirements of an organization. This requirement can be phrased in terms of a number of psychological dichotomies. An organization will continue only to the degree that there is both "conformity and nonconformity" (e.g., Campbell, 1961; Hollander and Willis, 1967; Rokeach, 1961), "remembering and forgetting" (e.g., McGlashan, 1967), or "destruction and creation of chaos" (e.g., Ashby, 1956). The reason for the instability of organizational arrangements, and the reason they must be continually reaccomplished, is that the requirements for flexibility and stability are mutually exclusive. The attainment of one is at the expense of the other. Flexibility is required to modify current practices so that nontransient changes in the environment can be adapted to. This means that the organization must detect changes and retain a sufficient pool of novel responses to accommodate to these changes. But total flexibility makes it impossible for the organization to retain a sense of identity and continuity. Any social unit is defined in part by its history, by what it has done repeatedly and chosen repeatedly. Stability also provides an economical means to handle new contingencies; there are regularities which an organization can exploit *if* it has a memory and the capacity for repetition. But total adherence to past wisdom would be as disruptive as total flexibility, because more economical ways of responding would never be discovered and new environmental features would seldom be noticed.

An organization can reconcile the need for flexibility with the need for stability in several ways: by some form of compromise response (a solution which is tried too often with much too disastrous results), by alternation between stability and flexibility, or by simultaneous expression of the two necessities in different portions of the system. As will be argued later, only in the second two cases is continued existence possible. A compromise response accomplishes neither flexibility nor stability.

7.   *Organizing is directed toward removing equivocality from the informational environment.*   The basic raw materials on which organizations operate are informational inputs that are ambiguous, uncertain, equivocal. Whether the information is embedded in tangible raw materials, recalcitrant customers, assigned tasks, or union demands, there are many possibilities, or sets of outcomes that *might* occur. Organizing serves to narrow the range of possibilities, to reduce the number of "might occurs." The activities of organizing are directed toward the establishment of a workable level of certainty. An organization attempts to transform equivocal information into a degree of unequivocality with which it can work and to which it is accustomed. This means that absolute certainty is seldom required. It also means that there can be enormous differences among organizations and industries with respect to the level of clarity that they regard as sufficient for action.

But even more important for an understanding of organizations is the fact that it takes equivocality to remove equivocality, or as Ashby's Law of Requisite Variety (1956) states, it takes variety to destroy variety. This means that processes must have the same degree of order or chaos as there is in the input to these processes. If an orderly process is applied to a chaotic set of information inputs, then only a small portion of these inputs will be attended to and made unequivocal. The major portion of the equivocality in the input will remain outside the control of the system. To cite a minor example, there is the old situation in which a person complaining of a cold visits a doctor, who turns him away with the remark, "See me when you get pneumonia; I can treat that." The common cold is a complex, poorly understood set of equivocal symptoms controlled by an equivocal set of antecedents. When this equivocal "information" encounters unequivocal medical treatment, not much happens. Some of the equivocal features of the cold are made unequivocal (e.g., variable amounts of congestion are reduced and made stable), but in general the equivocal nature of the cold remains intact; it is left to "run its course." If, however, the medical treatment were more equivocal, then more of the equivocality in the cold could be removed. But just what does it mean to apply a "more equivocal treatment process"? An equivocal process consists of a set of actions whose interrelations are imperfectly conceived and whose outcomes are subject to two or more plausible interpretations. For a physician, an equivocal treatment method would involve his doing several things. The things he did would be related as pairs of events (e.g., one drug might stimulate, another might tranquilize), but the relations *among* the several pairs of actions would be unknown. The physician could make statements about the relationships within the different portions of what he did for the patient, but he could not articulate the interrelationships *among* the several portions. Whatever outcome resulted from the application of these practices could be explained plausibly in terms of different possible interrelationships that *could* have occurred among all the components. The physician couldn't know for certain which explanation was correct.

Equivocal processing could be described in a more colorful manner as the scrambling of a process. What this means is that some relationships already known to exist in the process are removed, or some relationships are added, without any knowledge of how this change will affect the other relationships in the process. In other words, the relationships in the process are disturbed either by removal or addition of some components. The relationship between any two elements that form a pair is *not* disturbed, but the complete pattern of relationships, which determines the outcome, is changed in some unknown way. As disorderly as all this appears, it is precisely this disordering that must occur in the process if a corresponding amount of disorder is to be removed from the input to the process. Rendering a process equivocal does not *guarantee* that equivocality will be removed from the input. But it does guarantee that the equivocality in the input will be registered accurately. And if it is registered accurately, there is a greater probability that more of the equivocality will undergo some form of change, and that the direction of this change will be from equivocal to unequivocal.

The point that the equivocality of processes must match the equivocality of their informational inputs can also be illustrated in terms of person perception. With respect to the ability of a person to comprehend accurately what another person is like, Allport makes the following assertion:

> As a rule people cannot comprehend others who are more complex and subtle than they. The single track mind has little feeling for the conflicts of the versatile mind. ... Would it not follow, therefore, that the psychiatrist, since he deals with intricate mental tangles, should benefit by the possession of a complex personality? If he has neurotic difficulties of his own and manages them well, might they not add to his qualifications?[1]

Restated in the terminology used here, psychiatric understanding improves to the extent that the equivocality in the person who processes information (the psychiatrist) matches the equivocality in the information produced by the patient.

To anticipate a later argument, the inability of organizations to tolerate equivocal processing may well be the most important reason why they have trouble. It is the unwillingness to meet equivocality in an equivocal manner that produces failure, nonadaptation, autism, isolation from reality, psychological cost, etc. It is the unwillingness to disrupt order, ironically, that makes it impossible for the organization to create order. Order consists of

---

[1]From G. W. Allport, *Pattern and Growth in Personality* (New York: Holt, Rinehart and Winston, 1961), p. 508. Reprinted by permission.

unequivocal information, but information never comes to us in this form. It comes in equivocal form and can become unequivocal only through the operation of processes that first register and then transform this equivocality. Accurate registering requires the matching of processes to the characteristics of their inputs. Only if this prior matching occurs is transformation possible. If human actors cherish the unequivocal and the methods which they think maintain it, then adaptation and survival become a distinct problem which they are unlikely to solve.

CHAPTER FOUR

Interlocked Behaviors: The Elements of Organizing

Organizing is accomplished by several recurrent processes, but before we can talk about the processes, we need to describe the elements of which they are composed. Processes consist of individual behaviors that are interlocked among two or more people. The behaviors of one person are contingent on the behaviors of another person(s), and it is this contingency, described earlier as the interact and double interact, which is the main property that separates collective from singular action.

The purpose of this chapter is to indicate one means by which interlocked behaviors can be conceptualized: Allport's (1962) concept of *collective structure*. The chapter also illustrates how this concept can be applied to the issue of compensation practices in industrial organizations. It is important for the reader to understand that we are equating the common term "organizational structure" with the notion of interlocked behaviors. The structure that determines what an organization does and how it appears is the same structure that is established by regular patterns of interlocked behaviors.

THE CONCEPT OF COLLECTIVE STRUCTURE

To get a feeling for Allport's concept of collective structure, consider the following question: When someone says that "the group imposes norms on its members," precisely what does the word "group" refer to? If it is not people who impose norms, then we are at a loss to know just who does impose them, and why these particular norms were chosen. The developmental sequence implied is that first a group forms and *then* there is a convergence on rules for maintaining the group. Allport suggests that it makes more sense to reverse this sequence. He argues that convergence *precedes,* and is a necessary condition for, the emergence of groups. Thus an initial overlap among people in their beliefs—an overlap which *looks like* behavior controlled by norms—makes it possible for more enduring social relationships to emerge. When two people encounter one another, there is some possibility that each can benefit the other. For each, the contact with another person affords the possibility of increased need-satisfaction and self-expression. But these opportunities can be preserved only if each can count on the continued presence of the other person. Note that a preliminary convergence of interest occurs because each anticipates that the other can benefit him and each has a similar notion of how this can be accomplished. Having *first* converged on shared ideas of how a structure can form, the persons *then* activate a repetitive cycle of interlocked behaviors—that is, they form a collective structure. The range of their behaviors narrows *before* a group forms, not after; the group is made possible by this narrowing and convergence. In Allport's words, whenever

> there is a pluralistic situation in which in order for an individual (or class of individuals) to perform some act (or have some experience) that he "desires" to perform (or for which he is "set") it is necessary that *another* person (or persons) perform certain acts (either similar or different and complementary to his own), we have what can be called a fact of collective structure. It is either collectively actualized or potential.[1]

After this overview, we can now explore in greater detail just what a collective structure is. Obviously, one crucial question is, "Why does a collective structure form?" If this question remains unanswered, it is superfluous to talk about groups in the language of collective structure, because all we gain is a bland description and yet another term.

Assume that change rather than stability is the rule. People are continually exposed to streams of ongoing events (Schutz, 1967). If change is so continuous, it becomes difficult for a person to make sense of what is happening and to anticipate what will happen *unless* he is able to make some of these events recur. If a person wants to make the world more predictable, then he has to establish events which terminate and are repeated. He has to stabilize some portion of the ongoing events. But in an interdependent world crowded with people, it is difficult to produce closure

---

[1]From F. H. Allport, "A Structuronomic Conception of Behavior: Individual and Collective," *Journal of Abnormal and Social Psychology, 64* (1962), p. 17. Reprinted by permission.

by solitary acts. Cycles can be established only if one takes account of other persons. To establish cycles with another person requires the discovery and implementation of one or more mutually reciprocal behaviors. The pattern of behaviors which fit the requirements of mutual reciprocity has been described most adequately by investigators using exchange models of social behavior (e.g., Blau, 1964; Homans, 1958; Longabaugh, 1966; Thibaut and Kelley, 1959). The behaviors which are most likely to produce closure in a series of changing events are behaviors which A emits that are valuable to B, and which in turn lead B to produce behaviors that benefit A. Once a set of these interlocking behaviors has been established, a collective structure exists. "The give-and-take of two reciprocating individuals . . . is a *cycle* in which the behavior of each receives closure from, and is bound through reciprocation to, the behavior of the other within a collective structure made up of the two" (Allport, 1962, p. 13).

While it may be sufficient to argue that collective structure emerges to produce order and regularity, there may be other reasons why collective structures emerge. If other persons are around, it is rewarding to them and to us to at least have our mutual presences acknowledged. Thus acknowledgment is both expected and valued. Reciprocal acknowledgment by itself constitutes an elementary form of collective structure, but one would hardly argue that by itself it is very important. However, once acknowledgment has occurred, the probability increases that other behaviors will be interlocked. Only if each person stays within the "range of stimulation" of the other will it be possible to discover additional, more valuable sets of articulated actions. This suggests a simple explanation for the recurrent finding that persons in close physical proximity over time develop liking for one another (e.g., Festinger, Schachter, and Back, 1950). Proximity aids the discovery and implementation of behaviors, other than those of acknowledgment, which can be interlocked to mutual advantage.

An appropriate question to insert at this point is, "How does this view help us define a group?" A common assertion about groups is that they are "more than the sum of their parts" or that "the group is an emergent level." The obvious problem here is that we have no idea just what it is that emerges. If there are different levels of analysis (e.g., individual, group, organization, society), the only way we can learn much about any of these levels is if we know how they are tied together, that is, how one level interacts with another level. This is the problem of composition laws (Brodbeck, 1958). Investigators are compelled to make some statement about the way in which levels are tied together, since the basic element at each level is still the individual. The advantage of Allport's formulation is that he is explicit about one way in which levels are linked. The concept of collective structure preserves both the fact that "lower" levels constrain "higher" levels and the fact that "higher" levels are distinct from "lower" levels.

To be more specific, the elements potentially available for a collective structure consist of the behaviors that can be produced by A and the behaviors that can be produced by B. The only possible source of these behaviors is the participants. It is in this sense that lower levels constrain higher levels. The collective structure can involve only those behaviors that A and B are capable of producing. A collective structure exists when behaviors of two or more persons become interstructured and repetitive. The unit of analysis now becomes the interact or double interact (e.g., Barker and Wright, 1955, p. 328) and *not* the act. To identify instances of collective structure, we look for instances in which, with regularity, A emits an act which is followed predictably by an act from B, and B's act then determines A's subsequent act.

Several implications and refinements of this concept can now be explored. It is vital to note that it is behaviors, not persons, that are interstructured. This fact is preserved in Allport's phrase, "partial inclusion." A person does not invest all his behavior in a single group; commitments and interlockings are dispersed among several groups. Once this point is recognized, then it is more apparent why some predictions about groups are not confirmed. The simple reason is that a member has interlocked fewer of his behaviors with other members than the investigator assumed. This is a persistent problem in the attraction and cohesion literature, for example. Several of these studies make the implicit assumption that if someone interacts with, helps, or agrees with you, then you will like *all* of him and will become wholly interdependent with him when performing joint tasks. But there is no reason to think that involvement is this complete. Reciprocities involve specific actions. And once a given reciprocity is established, other ones may or may not be established. It is possible that some person other than one's present partner might be more suitable for producing closure in other behaviors. The consequence is that some behaviors are interlocked with one person and some with another. It is in this sense that Thibaut and Kelley's (1959) concept of the Comparison Level for Alternatives (CL_{alt}) is partly correct and partly incomplete. The concept states that a group member has some standard of acceptable outcomes, such that if the outcomes he attains are above this point, he will be dependent on the group and will remain a member. However, if outcomes fall below this point, he will search for other groups where higher outcomes can be achieved. The value of this notion is that it helps to explain why groups form and disband, and why persons enter and leave. But the concept is incomplete because it is tied to people rather than behaviors. With respect to some behaviors, interlocking could yield outcomes above the CL_{alt}, but with regard to other behaviors, the same group might be inadequate to produce closure. Thus it is probable that, for any group member, some behaviors are above the CL_{alt} and some below. A literal application of Thibaut and Kelley's concept would suggest that the person would sum up all his current outcomes, good and bad, and on the basis of this sum would either stay or leave. Our point is that he may do *both*. He stays in the group in the sense that some of his behavior remains interlocked with its members, and at the same time he leaves the group in the sense that he looks outside for significant persons who can provide closure for other behaviors. Thus any person is typically a member of several groups; to predict his behavior in any one group, we must know the investment he has in the behaviors interlocked in that group *plus* the extent to which significant behaviors are tied elsewhere. Only if this information is available will it be possible to predict how much effort he will expend to preserve his ties with the group and how much energy he will put into the execution of group tasks.

Note that from this perspective one could argue that subjects in laboratory studies might have a *considerable* investment in temporary laboratory groups, especially if the groups perform intellectual tasks. The argument would be that among college subjects, it is important to demonstrate intelligence. If other members of the group permit the individual to act intelligently (i.e., ask for his ideas, give the ideas careful attention, criticize obvious errors), then he *has* tied an important behavior to other persons, even though this interlocking may be short-lived. He takes the group seriously because it takes a serious part of him seriously.

However, the concept of "partial inclusion" can be overemphasized, and one must be alert to a dynamic that works against it. Diffusion of behaviors among several relationships undoubtedly requires more energy and compartmentalization of interests than does the concentration of investments into a relatively small number of collectivities. Considerations of cognitive economy suggest that the fewer the persons with whom behaviors are tied, the easier it is to monitor and control the fate of these relationships.

A second point that must be stressed is that persons differ in their involvements in particular structures. Involvement can be assumed to be a direct function of the amount of closure that is produced by the reciprocal behavior and of the number and importance of rewards that are received. Involvement can be measured by the degree to which a person would invest effort to preserve a faltering collective structure.

This leads to the point that, once a structure is formed, people try to preserve it (Allport, 1962, p. 20). They look for and provide one another with "structural assurances." These are mutual indications that (1) the structure can be counted on and will continue to operate, and (2) each will retain his place in it.

The concept of collective structure by no means includes everything that is in a group. As should be apparent, there is virtually no end to the list of symptoms one could use to characterize a group. The relevant point about collective structure is that it is assumed to be a basic property of groups from which other properties derive. The concept retains the fact that groups are composed of individuals and that groups are defined in terms of observable behaviors, but it does not overlook the fact that groups are unique. The concept anchors this uniqueness in a property not found in isolated individuals, namely, repetitive interstructured behaviors.

This way of describing a group's uniqueness may cause some discomfort, because it implies that groups are somehow less substantial, less tangible, and less "dramatic" than many people presume. Groups, as we "know" them, somehow seem to disappear when they are described as sets of interstructured behaviors. To some extent, groups *are* less distinctive than people have imagined. People have erroneously assumed that persons, rather than behaviors, constitute the group. Furthermore, many of the things that people have labeled as unique in groups often turn out to be (1) fictitious in the sense that they are not observable, (2) derivable from the fact that behaviors are interlocked, or (3) individual attributes that have been erroneously attributed to the group (e.g., cohesion is really a liking by individuals for individuals).

COLLECTIVE STRUCTURE IN THE LABORATORY

A further idea of how collective structure develops can be gained from a laboratory technology developed by Sidowski (1957), which preserves the majority of features implicit in the concept of collective structure. This technology is labeled the "minimal social situation," and the extensions of it by Kelley and his associates are of particular relevance for us. The situation is best characterized as austere. Two persons are put in separate rooms, without knowledge of each other's presence. Each can press one of two buttons which control the outcomes of the *other* person. One button delivers a punishment, the other a reward. Neither person controls his own outcomes directly, but he does affect what happens to the other person. The question is this: is it possible, and if so under what conditions, for two persons to arrive at a "mutually advantageous" solution, in which each receives rewards and avoids punishments? Studies (Kelley, Thibaut, Radloff, and Mundy, 1962; Rabinowitz, Kelley, and Rosenblatt, 1966) show that persons *are* able to produce mutually advantageous interactions, a fact that in itself is surprising since the relationship develops "*unconsciously* (without realization of the relationship), *unintentionally* (without deliberately planning to do so), and *tacitly* (without words or speech)" (Rabinowitz, Kelley, and Rosenblatt, 1966, p. 194). Recently, an important set of studies involving the minimal social situation has made considerable progress in specifying the conditions under which this mutually profitable interchange can be established. Rabinowitz, Kelley, and Rosenblatt (1966) found that discovery of solutions is a function of the pattern of interdependence and the conditions of response timing that prevail between the two persons. When the two persons are in the pattern of interdependence labeled mutual fate control (each person has complete control over the other's outcomes), mutually advantageous solutions are more likely if the responses of the two persons are synchronized rather than randomly timed. However, when the two persons are in a relationship where one has fate control and the other has behavioral control (the person with behavioral control is in a position to control the actions of the other person but not his outcomes), then there is a greater likelihood that they will arrive at a mutually advantageous solution if their responses are unsynchronized.

The distinction between fate control and behavioral control can be illustrated in terms of the two components of the minimal social situation, the behavior of button pressing and the outcomes of either reward or punishment. Fate control occurs when person A controls the outcomes for person B. Regardless of which button B presses, he will receive either a reward or punishment depending on which button A pushes. B's fate is totally in the hands of A, and he can do nothing to change this fate. Mutual fate control means that A has this kind of control over B, and B has this kind of control over A.

In a situation of behavioral control, the behavior of button pressing is controlled directly and the outcomes are controlled indirectly. If A has behavioral control over B, whenever A pushes a button B will receive *either* a reward or punishment depending on which button he himself presses. A does not control B's final outcome directly, but A's action does determine which of B's buttons will deliver a reward and which will deliver a punishment. Thus A does exert some control over B, because over time B will press repeatedly the button which gives him good outcomes and will avoid pressing the button that gives him bad outcomes.

With these examples of patterns of interdependence in mind, we can now discuss the fit between the minimal social situation and the concept of collective structure. The emergence of mutually advantageous solutions we take to be a prototypic instance of collective structure. A mutually rewarding, reciprocal set of behaviors has become interstructured; and once this structure is discovered, it tends to persist. The fact that the structure was created unconsciously is no problem; the Allport formulation does not require that the members be conscious that a collective structure is emerging—in fact, Allport argues that the strength of the bond may be more intense if it is formed outside of awareness (1962, p. 13). The minimal social situation as it has been used by Kelley supplements the analysis of Allport because it suggests some antecedents that control the emergence of collective structure, namely, response pacing and the pattern of interdependence. The Kelley research also makes the important point that collective structure is *not* inevitable whenever two persons are in the presence of one another. Profitable exchanges were *not* always established in the laboratory experiments. And when they were, they did not operate with total efficiency or stability. In part, this could be explained by the fact that the laboratory rewards probably were less important than are those to which Allport alludes. But this is probably a difference in degree rather than kind. It does appear that the minimal social situation incorporates, in a highly controlled and visible setting, the crucial properties of collective structure discussed by Allport. The advantage of the laboratory is that we can now ask more pointed questions about the origins and permanence of collective structure, and the effects of this structure on productivity.

The reader at this point may be having considerable difficulty in seeing the relevance of this technique or line of theorizing for the problems of organizations. A partial answer to this puzzlement is simply that the minimal social situation represents a clear instance in which a potentially significant property of organizations has been stripped of its managerial significance and terminology, in the interest of generating theory. In the next section, we trace some implications of this analysis for the organizationally relevant question of the effects of wages on productivity.

THE EFFECTS OF WAGES ON COLLECTIVE STRUCTURE

So far, it has been shown that response pacing and the pattern of interdependence affect the likelihood that a stable collective structure will emerge. The question can then be asked, "How do differences in wages affect response pacing and interdependence?" To answer this question, we must first look at wages in terms of the concept of collective structure and then look at wages in terms of the minimal social situation and the findings reported by Kelley.

With respect to the formation of a collective structure, wages might be relevant because they influence the hierarchy of behaviors that are available for incorporation into a collective structure. When wage issues are salient, the worker may anticipate that certain outcomes will occur if he obtains a certain level of wages. Following the model proposed by Cofer and Appley (1964), we could argue that the anticipation of these outcomes leads to the invigoration of some subset of behaviors. Now, if the reader will tolerate a phrase that is more picturesque than precise, what we have is a "set of invigorated behaviors in search of a closure person." Undoubtedly, most of the behaviors that are invigorated require some kind of reciprocal response from another person(s) if they are to be executed. It is these behaviors, and the performer's desire to establish a self-closing, dependable cycle for them, which set the stage for the formation of a collective structure. The highest behavior in the person's hierarchy is the one that is most likely to become linked with the behavior of another person. In other words, assuming that money crystallizes some hierarchy of behaviors, it is the behaviors at the top of this hierarchy which will probably be the ones that the person tries to engage in a collective structure. At least two obvious ramifications are suggested. First, if the behavior which is highest in the hierarchy does elicit a reciprocal response from another person, the first person's involvement in this particular collective structure should be high. The interlocked behaviors produce closure around an issue that is important to him. However, if the person forms a collective structure using some behavior much lower in his hierarchy, then we would expect that his involvement would be less and the collective structure more fleeting. It might also be argued that behaviors which are high in the hierarchy serve as a "search rule." A worker may explore the population of people in his immediate situation and try to determine which of these people will produce a behavior that will enable him to achieve closure. The worker does much more than simply look around for someone with whom he can compare his accomplishments (Festinger, 1954). He is actually looking for someone who can make it possible for accomplishments to occur. Without reciprocity most invigorated behaviors will not complete a cycle and will not be viewed as accomplishments.

Now it is possible to make a bridge from collective structure to the minimal social situation. There is some evidence (Katz, 1964; Opsahl and Dunnette, 1966) to indicate that individual incentives lead to a higher rate of effort expenditure than do group incentives, and that piece rate wages may produce a higher rate of responding than do hourly wages. These findings are of interest because they concern the emission of responses. If money produces a high rate of response emission, then it is *less* likely that a person will form a collective structure if he is in a mutual fate control relationship, but *more* likely if he is in a relationship of fate control-behavioral control. The assumption here is that high rates of response emission make it more difficult to synchronize responses. And as the analysis by Kelley demonstrates, in the absence of synchrony, mutual fate control relationships rarely lead to the development of a collective structure; fate control-behavioral control relationships, on the other hand, develop into collective structures more readily if there is no synchrony. We can go one step further. It is possible that when money produces unsynchronized responses in the mutual fate control relationship, and thus thwarts the development of collective structure, the persons are placed in a situation of high ambiguity. It becomes more difficult for them to establish reciprocal and dependable relationships. Given that such ambiguity is bothersome and leads to idiosyncratic responding (Lazarus, 1966, p. 118), then it might be expected that productivity would become more variable (e.g., Shapiro and Leiderman, 1967).

Besides affecting response pacing, money might also be crucial because it affects the pattern of interdependence which exists between persons. Differential payment of persons may generate either a relationship of mutual fate control or a mixed relationship of fate control and behavioral control. Given the existence of these patterns of interdependence, then the question is, "Which pattern of interdependence does the rate of response emission in the work situation favor?" If it favors the existing pattern of interdependence, then collective structures are more likely to occur.

It is also possible that a person's knowledge of his own relationship with other people and his cognitions about the situation could influence his choice of partner for a collective structure. Suppose that a person possesses a unique set of skills, a set that is valuable and is difficult for anyone else in the organization to duplicate. The person could legitimately conclude that he has fate control over several persons in the organization. He can control whether they obtain good or bad outcomes. Now suppose that he has the choice to interact either with a person who would also exert fate control over him or with a person who would exert behavioral control over him. Our prediction would be that he would prefer that colleague whose form of reciprocal power would *match* the response pacing requirements of the situation. He would prefer a colleague to have fate control over him if the situation provided ample opportunities to synchronize responses, but he would prefer a colleague with behavioral control if the situation afforded less opportunity for synchrony. In other words, he would choose that person with whom he had a higher probability of establishing an enduring collective structure. Of course, we could also turn this around and argue that in a given relationship, such as mutual fate control, the person would control his rate of response emission in such a way as to heighten the chances that an interlocking set of behaviors would be created. For example, if a person is constrained to a relationship of mutual fate control, we would expect that he would try to fit the pace of his responses to that of his partner. In this way he would increase the chances that they would discover a mutually rewarding set of contingencies. On the other hand, if the relationship consisted of fate control-behavioral control, then he might engage in more unsynchronized responding.

To summarize this illustration, the basic idea is that when money is offered, persons anticipate certain outcomes. This anticipation serves to energize a set of behaviors, most of which have interpersonal implications. That is, most behaviors that are evoked require the assistance of other people if they are to be carried to completion. This assistance takes the form of responses which facilitate the completion of the behavior. But the response by the other person must be "bought at a price." The person who wishes to execute the behavior must make it worthwhile for the other person to give support. Undoubtedly, people prefer enduring support to temporary support, and for this reason they have some interest in producing a viable collective structure. The behaviors that are made salient by the anticipations are the ones that are most likely to become engaged in a collective structure. As the collective structure forms, the person simultaneously acts to perform his assigned task(s). We have not described, however, the precise nature of the linkage between collective structure and action, partly because it makes a difference for productivity precisely which behaviors become interstructured. Our analysis suggests that either task-related or task-irrelevant behaviors could be the basis for collective structure. Whatever behaviors become interstructured, we would expect this structure to be protected by the participants so long as it remains rewarding. Another reason why we cannot be precise at this stage about implications for productivity is that we have said that behaviors, not people, are interstructured. Before we could make accurate predictions regarding productivity, we would have to know the structures in which a person's other behaviors were embedded, the importance of those structures, and the ways in which they were interrelated.

CHAPTER FIVE

The Processes of Organizing

The interlocked behaviors discussed in the previous chapter are the basic elements which are combined in different ways to compose the processes that accomplish organizing. Each process involved in organizing contains sets of interlocked behaviors that may remove some equivocality from information that is fed into that process. What we now have to specify is just what these processes involve. We know that a process contains "families" of interlocked behaviors, that the behaviors which compose a specific process are similar in some ways, and that this similarity distinguishes one process from another. But we have not described the specific processes involved in organizing, nor have we described how a process operates. This chapter describes the types of processes involved in organizing, and the next chapter describes the inner workings of each process.

Some insight into the possible processes that can accomplish organizing is provided by existing theories of sociocultural evolution (e.g., Campbell, 1959, 1965a, 1965b). In this chapter we will discuss the processes that are assumed to operate in sociocultural evolution, and the ways in which these processes need to be amended for inclusion in organization theory. The reader should understand that it is processes of evolution, *not* outcomes of these processes, in which we are interested. We are not interested in what is evolved, but rather in how evolution occurs. Furthermore, the processes are not assumed to be lodged in particular parts of the organization. An individual or a group may engage in all the processes, or different groups may perform different processes. In all likelihood, formal organizations are characterized by the latter possibility, but that is not crucial to the argument.

THE SOCIOCULTURAL EVOLUTION MODEL

Donald T. Campbell has been perhaps the most vigorous contemporary exponent of an evolutionary model adapted to social behavior, and this section relies heavily on his thinking. The following excerpt provides an overview of the evolutionary form of analysis.

> For an evolutionary process to take place there need to be variations (as by mutation, trial, etc.), stable aspects of the environment differentially selecting among such variations and a retention-propagation system rigidly holding on to the selected variations. The variation and the retention aspects are inherently at odds. Every new mutation represents a failure of reproduction of a prior selected form. Too high a mutation rate jeopardizes the preservation of already achieved adaptations. There arise in evolutionary systems, therefore, mechanisms for curbing the variation rate. The more elaborate the achieved adaptation, the more likely are mutations to be deleterious, and therefore the stronger the inhibitions on mutation. For this reason we may expect to find great strength in the preservation and propagation systems, which will lead to a perpetuation of once-adaptive traits long after environmental shifts have removed their adaptedness.[1]

The essential ideas in the preceding quotation are: (1) three processes—variation, selection, and retention—are responsible for evolution; (2) variations in behaviors and genetic mutations are haphazard, and those variations are selected and retained that receive greater reinforcement or provide for greater survival; (3) the processes of variation and retention are opposed, the same point made earlier (see p. 39) regarding flexibility and stability; (4) resort to a concept such as "plan" or "external guidance" is unnecessary to explain the course of evolution; (5) moderate rates of mutation are necessary for survival and for evolutionary advantage. To gain a more complete understanding of evolution, we will briefly discuss each of the three processes.

Variation is perhaps the most obvious feature that characterizes sociocultural as well as biological evolution. Variations at the sociocultural level can occur between social groups, between members within a single group, or across the different occasions when a single group acts. In general, it is assumed that "the more numerous and the greater the heterogeneity of variations, the richer the opportunities for an advantageous innovation"

---

[1]From D. T. Campbell, "Ethnocentric and Other Altruistic Motives." In D. Levine (Ed.), *Nebraska Symposium on Motivation, 1965* (Lincoln: Univ. of Nebraska Press, 1965). Quote is reprinted by permission from pp. 306-307.

(Campbell, 1965b, p. 28). Haphazard variation, as opposed to rational variation, is emphasized in evolutionary theory. While it might appear that "intelligent" variation is to be preferred, the reader can recall that this form of variation is restricted largely to wisdom that has already been achieved. A person can intelligently suggest some innovation that he has encountered before, but since his experiences are limited, this form of variation is also limited. Note that the occurrence of blind variation provides a plausible explanation for the finding that groups often seem to be "wiser" than any of their members. In biological evolution, selection creates novelty by compounding various genotypes. Similarly, by combining different portions of responses produced by different members, it is possible for a group to reinforce and establish composite solutions and modes of behavior which no single member was capable of producing by himself.

A final point that must be emphasized concerning variation is that a response must occur at least once before it can be available for selection. This apparently obvious fact has sizable implications. The argument is stated this way: "the entire repertoire of an individual or species must exist prior to . . . selection but only in the form of minimal units" (Skinner, 1966, p. 1206). The response does not necessarily have to be emitted in its completed form, but something must be made available that can be shaped over time into an adaptive response. The importance of this argument lies in the idea that all the forms of behavior we observe in a surviving system, regardless of their apparent value at the present time, were at one time emitted in some more primitive form and then gradually shaped over time into their present form. The contingencies in the environment that shaped a response are the crucial ones for explaining its origin. In a real sense the response is under the control of those stimuli responsible for the shaping, rather than the stimuli that now make it appropriate. What this means, then, is that the response is apt to be quite stubborn. It would extinguish very slowly if the present stimuli that reinforce it were removed. To speed up extinction, it would be essential that all the associations between the response and the stimuli *responsible for its shaping* also be removed (Rohde, 1967).

The *selection* process is considerably more complicated than variation. It is so complex that many researchers think it cannot be applied to groups. Their objection is that "selection" can occur in so many ways that the concept does not explain very much of what happens. It is easy to attribute everything that occurs to some kind of selection, and for this reason the explanation loses its power. There is also the danger of circular thinking. We observe the outcome of a supposed selection process and "explain" the existence of this outcome by saying that it was selected. But to the question, "How do you know it was selected?" the answer often is, "Because it is there." It is there because it was selected, it was selected because it is there. Thus one must be very careful to specify the selection system and its outcomes *independently,* and avoid the temptation to infer the selection system from the outcomes it produces.

Campbell discusses selective systems and selective criteria separately. He suggests that there are at least six selective systems that can be observed in sociocultural evolution.

1. *Selective survival of complete social organizations.* This is the most direct parallel between biological and social evolution. This is the situation in which entire societies or large portions of them may have been eliminated because they were unfit for efficient collective action.

2. *Selective diffusion among groups.* This selection system is the *least* direct parallel between biological and social evolution, because borrowing is impossible in gene systems. The essence of this system is that behaviors characteristic of prosperous groups are borrowed by groups which are less prosperous.

3. *Selective perpetuation of temporal variations.* As a group performs different actions over time, different memories of pleasure and pain will be associated with these actions, and pleasurable actions will be repeated more often than painful ones.

4. *Selective imitation of interindividual variations.* Just as groups may imitate other groups, members within one group may imitate the actions of other members of that same group. The psychological processes of conformity and imitation describe this form of borrowing.

5. *Selective promotion to leadership roles.* A further mechanism by which certain variations may be singled out for perpetuation is the promotion mechanism. The group singles out persons who vary customary practices in ways which appear more adaptive, and then elevates these persons to positions of authority.

6. *Rational selection.* Societies do plan, forecast, and anticipate. For the sake of completeness we will include this form of selection, even though it is relatively unimportant.

The selection process contains one or more of these six mechanisms. They are the media through which selection criteria operate.

Selection criteria appear to be almost infinite in number. In the case of organizations, one can think of numerous decision premises (Simon, 1957) that serve as selection criteria: accept that which brings pleasure, reject that which brings pain; accept prompt responses, reject slow responses; accept a novel response, reject a conventional response; accept the rational, reject the irrational. But even though criteria are abundant, one need not assume that an infinite number are used. Furthermore, it is probable that criteria exist in hierarchies, so that some are more important and applied more frequently than others.

Perhaps the most stubborn problem with selection criteria is that social systems use two types of criteria: criteria relevant to the internal functioning of the system, and criteria relevant to the external functioning of the system with its environment. And it is entirely possible that internal criteria are applied more frequently than are external criteria. Even more crucial is the fact that successful application of internal selectors may provide the illusion that all is going well when in fact the group has paid virtually no attention to the changing environment. Internal criteria are concerned mainly with the stability of the system. Habit meshing (Campbell, 1965b, p. 33) is an example:

> A process of habit meshing takes place within any organization, in that each person's habits are a part of the environment of others. Encounters which are punishing tend to extinguish [the habit]. ... Rewarding encounters increase the strength of behavioral tendencies on the part of both parties. Thus any social organization tends to move in the direction of internal compatibility, *independently of increased adaptiveness* [italics added].

If this discussion of habit meshing is placed alongside the earlier discussion of interlocking, it can be seen that successful interlocking (habit meshing) can occur without any necessary increase in the productivity or viability of the system.

The final evolutionary process is *retention*. Despite the fact that retention appears to be a straightforward storage process, it has more importance for human organizations than may be realized. For example, it was noted earlier that one would "expect the greatest rigidity, the greatest demand for conformity, [in] ... those societies with the more elaborate adaptive systems, particularly when these systems demand restraint on individual hedonistic impulse" (Campbell, 1965b, p. 34). The reason for this prediction is that elaborate adaptation systems are vulnerable to mutations; they are held in place by complex forces which can easily be destroyed, and one of the principal threats is persons acting in terms of self-preservation rather than group preservation.

Retention systems are not simply repositories for behaviors that have been selected. They affect subsequent actions; they are frequently edited; they are protected in elaborate ways that may conflict with variation and selection; they are coercive only to the degree that members are informed of their contents; and they contain items that frequently are opposed to the self-interest of persons who must implement these items. Retained contents can also be internally inconsistent. This point is crucial. The selection system operates in terms of contemporary inputs, a psychological here and now, and items which are selected for retention may contradict items that were stored previously. Thus to understand the working of evolutionary processes within organizations, it may be necessary to posit internal reorganization in the retention system, even though such reorganization is not given central attention in biological versions of evolutionary theory.

AMENDMENTS TO EVOLUTIONARY THEORY

If we wish to use portions of the theory of sociocultural evolution to understand more about organizing, then some revisions are necessary to make the theory compatible with the properties of organizations. Some of these amendments have already been hinted at (e.g., the necessity to posit internal reorganization in the retention process). In this section we will discuss some necessary changes in the concepts of choice points, orderly trial and error, adaptation, and the enacted environment.

Choice Points

Our description of evolutionary theory made little mention of choice in the determination of evolutionary processes. Deliberate rational variation was seen to be of limited value, and rational selection was described as a peripheral selection system. Yet it remains true that the capacity for choice is perhaps the most distinguishing property of human actors (Bertalanffy, 1967; Glasser, 1965; Jones and Gerard, 1967; Temerlin, 1963). It is possible at the sociocultural level for actors to modify the ways in which processes unfold, and to control at least some portions of the evolutionary sequence. The precise location of these choice points is open to question. However, it is conceivable that choice points in the evolutionary process are located on the output side of the retention system.

One can argue that there are two separate choices that occur once an evolutionary sequence has been completed: a noticing choice and a doing choice. Assume that some action has been selected and retained. The *noticing choice* can be phrased this way: "Knowing what I know now, should I notice something that I didn't notice before, and should I ignore something I noticed before?" This is a choice with respect to the selection process; it concerns whether or not the actor should revise his selection criteria. We assume that any item which is retained contains "surplus meaning." The item was originally retained for a specific reason, namely, that it provided some apparent advantage. But the item has *additional* implications that may have gone unnoticed at the moment it was selected. For example, suppose that within a problem-solving group it is discovered that talkative members increase the probability that good solutions will be produced. In subsequent personnel decisions, talkative people are recruited, and taciturn ones are rejected. Talkativeness thus gets incorporated as a selection criterion. But this criterion will be confounded, because several additional qualities will be retained along with the obvious property of talkativeness. Hoffman (1965, p. 106) has demonstrated that talkative people are characterized by what he labels the GAS syndrome; they are high in General

Activity, Ascendance, and Sociability, but not necessarily in other cognitive abilities. The GAS syndrome thus constitutes the "surplus meaning" that is retained when the quality of talkativeness is selected. This surplus meaning could at some future time affect the selection criteria that are used. It is available for reflection and for subsequent use.

Although this discussion of surplus meaning may sound exceedingly complex, all we are suggesting is that the actor is capable of reviewing decisions that have been made, and that in doing so he may discover properties he didn't notice earlier. He can then revise subsequent choices on the basis of this review. Thus the gross selection criterion of talkativeness could be refined in terms of one or more of its components. For example, it may be discovered on reflection that talkative people are high in sociability. It may then be assumed that sociability is the crucial behavior that produces good solutions (because, for instance, it reduces interpersonal tensions and allows better concentration); in this way the gross criterion of talkativeness could be replaced by the more refined criterion of sociability. The actor in this situation would act on the basis of what he knew and would make the choice to revise the criteria in the selection system.

The *doing choice* involves the same properties. It is phrased as follows: "Knowing what I know now, should I act differently?" This choice also depends on the retention system and the surplus meaning in the items it retains. But whereas the noticing choice involved a revision in selection criteria, the doing choice refers to a revision in the repertoire of responses that are produced—in other words, a revision in the variation process rather than the selection process. This means that variation can either be reduced ("I will do what I did before") or increased ("I will *not* do what I did before"). In either case, the variation process is influenced by the retention process, and this influence may be volitional. The human actor can choose whether the information that he retains will constrain or set free his subsequent actions. The doing choice is assumed to be independent of the noticing choice, even though both choices are tied to the retention process. They differ in that they affect different processes in the evolutionary sequence.

Whenever the actor decides to change either his selection criteria or his actions, he *discredits* some portion of his retained wisdom. When the selection criterion was changed from talkativeness to sociability, some previous knowledge was discredited. One already "knew" that talkativeness was important, but when the selection criterion was revised the importance of talkativeness was reduced. The same discrediting occurs when actions are revised. This is precisely what was implied in the sentence on page 55 which read, "Every new mutation represents a failure of reproduction of a prior selected form." Thus, even if we introduce choice into the evolutionary model, as we must in order to take account of human actors, this does not reduce the relevance of the evolutionary perspective.

Orderly Trial and Error

A second necessary amendment concerns blind, haphazard variation. Haphazard variation is unlikely to be prominent in sociocultural evolution for several reasons. In the first place, the instruction "be random" is a paradoxical injunction. If the person complies with it, he is not acting randomly. In the second place, it is difficult for people to sustain random responding. Whenever they attempt to do so, their actions soon fall into orderly patterns. The fact that they may be unaware of the pattern is irrelevant. It can no longer be characterized as blind and haphazard because it is orderly. In the third place, past knowledge always imposes some constraints on subsequent actions, even if the person is not conscious of the constraint (Skinner, 1966). But perhaps most crucial is the fact that random trial and error cannot explain some outcomes of evolutionary processes. These outcomes can be explained only if we assume that the variations were orderly. Although this is a complex point, it is important that we try to understand it.

The argument against the transformation of random mutations into elements that exhibit organized complexity is that a state of organized complexity can be reached by only a limited number of paths. These paths are determined by preexisting relationships inherent in matter inself. A glib application of the evolutionary argument would state that spontaneously arising, chaotic, primeval living matter evolved into complex organisms when the more successful and complex mutations of this matter were selected. But this type of selection is unlikely, because the necessary relationships for this evolution must exist *before* the particular elements can be selected and synthesized. Bertalanffy writes:

> Even if complex molecules like nucleoproteins and enzymes are considered as being "given," there is no known principle of physics and chemistry which, in reactions at random, would favor their "survival" against their decay; rather this is contrary to the second law of thermodynamics according to which a "soup" containing proteins, nucleoproteins, enzymes, etc., would tend to chemical equilibrium, that is, breakdown of "improbable" proteins, etc., into "probable" simple compounds (as happens after the death of any living system). Selection, i.e. favored survival of "better" precursors of life, already presupposes self-maintaining, complex, open systems which may compete; therefore selection cannot account for the origin of such systems.[2]

To state this argument more succinctly, one must posit that in the beginning there was organization, not chaos. Only if order is taken as a first principle, and the principles of organization *per se* are discovered, is it

---

[2]From L. von Bertalanffy, *Robots, Men, and Minds* (New York: Braziller, 1967), p. 82. Copyright © 1967 by Ludwig von Bertalanffy. Reprinted by permission of the publisher.

possible to make sense of evolutionary development. Principles of organization and relationship could not have evolved; they had to exist in some form from the beginning. Such a statement is not mystical or metaphysical. It simply says that entities are caused neither by some vitalistic force nor by accident. Instead, entities are formed and structured according to certain laws, and the important laws are laws of relationships and organization. Phrased in another way, the important question is, "what is the 'grammar' that gives order to the 'vocabulary' associated with human groups?" The grammar will consist of regulative and organizational properties that indicate why groups take various forms and why different mutations are not equally probable.

It has been demonstrated over and over that, if one knows the elements available and the rules by which they combine, then the precise outcome can be predicted. It is the interaction of rules and elements that determines the final outcome (e.g., Maruyama, 1963). And all we are saying here is that rules, not chance, determined the course of evolution, and that the important questions concern the nature of these rules and how, in interaction with specified elements, they produced viable structures. This is also why we have said repeatedly that to understand organizing is to understand organization. Organizing is the set of rules by which elements interact in predictable fashion with predictable outcomes. Organizing is the grammar by which the vocabulary of elements in an organization is made meaningful.

Adaptation and Selection

The third amendment concerns the necessity for separating selection from adaptation. A frequent assertion in evolutionary theory is that the progression from simpler forms to more complex forms was made in the common interest of improved adaptation and selective advantage. However, there are numerous instances in which selected items are *non*adaptive. For example, Skinner interprets the existence of superstitious behavior as an indication that selection and adaptation do not necessarily coincide:

> Behavior may have advantages which have played no role in its selection. The converse is also true. Events which follow behavior but are not necessarily produced by it may have a selective effect. ... All current characteristics of an organism do not necessarily contribute to its survival and procreation, yet they are all nevertheless "selected." Useless structures with associated useless functions are as inevitable as superstitious behavior. Both become more likely as organisms become more sensitive to contingencies.[3]

---

[3]From B. F. Skinner, "The Phylogeny and Ontogeny of Behavior," *Science, 153* (September 9, 1966), p. 1207. Copyright 1966 by the American Association for the Advancement of Science. Reprinted by permission.

The circumstance of superstitious behavior arises when an organism, receiving reinforcement on a fixed interval scale (every 30 seconds for example), typically repeats the pattern of behaviors present before the reinforcement is produced, whatever the pattern may be (e.g., jumping, turning around, walking away from the food place, etc.). An analogous situation occurs in groups in the form of confounded feedback (e.g., Hall, 1957; Zander and Wolfe, 1964). Whenever the different members of a group contribute portions of a finished product, and the group is given feedback about performance only in terms of the group product (e.g., it is acceptable, it is unacceptable), individual members have no way of knowing how adequate their *individual* contributions were. If the outcome is judged acceptable, this could mean that individual members will repeat their actions even if they were actually irrelevant or detrimental to the outcome. Thus we would have yet another instance in which certain behavior was selected (reinforced due to the success of the group) without any relation to adaptation.

Note the final sentence in the quotation from Skinner. It says that as sensitivity increases, there is greater likelihood that superstitious behavior will develop. Or stated in another way, the greater the sensitivity of the actor to contingencies in his environment, the greater the likelihood that his selected behaviors may be nonadaptive or irrelevant to adaptation. In the case of human actors this should be a persistent problem. In terms of the notion of retrospective meaning, when an actor attempts to determine what has occurred and why it has occurred, his explanation may well be erroneous and he may persist in his nonadaptive responses. The point we wish to make here is simply that selection processes are not infallible, and that selection can hinder adaptation as well as promote it. This point can be appreciated only if we free ourselves from the notion that selection is for environmental advantage.

The Enacted Environment

Although one of the central propositions in any evolutionary theory concerns the continuing press of the environment on the organism, the precise nature of this environment is never made explicit. This lack of clarity is especially troublesome when we begin to think of human organizations within an evolutionary framework. If we review the preceding amendments, it soon becomes clear that they have something to do with the ways in which environments are discussed. It has been mentioned that variations retain some orderliness, that information is the commodity processed in human systems, and that information retained by the actor may then constrain his subsequent actions. These subtle features of human organizing are difficult to fit into the gross portraits of the environment which are associated with evolutionary theory. We need a more explicit statement of what constitutes the environment of an organization, and we need to be certain that this portrait is consistent with what is known about the ways in which human beings function.

Instead of discussing the "external environment," we will discuss the "enacted environment." The phrase "enacted environment" preserves the crucial distinctions that we wish to make, the most important being that the human *creates* the environment to which the system then adapts. The human actor does not *re*act to an environment, he *en*acts it. It is this enacted environment, and nothing else, that is worked upon by the processes of organizing.

The concept of an enacted environment derives from a number of sources, including Mead (1956), Allport (1967), Skinner (1963, 1966), Bem (1965, 1967), Garfinkel (1967), Schachter (1967), and especially Schutz (1967), whose concepts comprise the bulk of this discussion.

To understand the crucial features of an enacted environment, one must cultivate an exquisite sensitivity to time. The chapter in which Schutz develops the most important portions of his analysis is entitled, "Meaningful Lived Experience." The importance of this title resides in the fact that it is phrased in the past tense: the meaningful experience is lived; it is not living or to be lived. This is the most crucial feature of the enacted environment. Stated bluntly, we can know what we've done only after we've done it. Only by doing is it possible for us to discover what we have done. One can also state this in stimulus-response language: only when a response has been completed does the stimulus become defined.

To understand these statements is to understand time. Time exists in two distinct forms, as pure duration and as discrete segments with spatio-temporal properties. Pure duration can be described in any one of a number of ways, the most useful being a stream of experience. Note that experience is stated in the singular, not the plural. To talk about experiences implies discrete, separate contents, and pure duration does not have this property. Pure duration is a "coming-to-be and passing-away that has no contours, no boundaries, and no differentiations" (Schutz, 1967, p. 47). The reader may object that his experience seldom has this quality of continual flowing, merging, and melting of phases into phases. In fact, experience as we know it has the quality of discreteness, separateness, the quality of being bounded and distinct. But the only way we get this impression is by stepping outside the stream of experience and directing attention to it. It is only possible to direct attention to what has already passed; it is impossible to direct attention to what is yet to come. All knowing and meaning arise from reflection, from a backward glance. The workings of the reflective glance can be glimpsed in the following quotation:

When, by my act of reflection, I turn my attention to my living experience, I am no longer taking up my position within the stream of pure duration, I am no longer simply living within that flow. The experiences are apprehended, distinguished, brought into relief, marked out from one another; the experiences which were constituted as phases within the flow of duration now become objects of attention as constituted experiences. What had first been constituted as a phase now stands out as a full-blown experience, no matter whether the Act of attention is one of reflection or of reproduction. ... *For the Act of attention*—and this is of major importance for the study of meaning—presupposes an elapsed, passed-away experience—in short, one that is already in the past.[4]

Given this concept of time, several properties of an enacted environment now become apparent. First, the creation of meaning is an attentional process, but it is attention to that which has already occurred. Second, since the attention is directed backward from a specific point in time (a specific here and now), whatever is occurring at the moment will influence what the person discovers when he glances backward. A complete formulation of meaning that preserves these features is "here, now, and thus." Attention is directed backward from a given point in time (here and now), and whatever past experiences it fixes on are the meaningful objects (thus). Third, the quotation from Schutz makes it apparent that memory processes, whether they be retention or reconstruction, influence meaning. Fourth, we can now see why it is that only when a response occurs does the stimulus become defined. The reason is that we cannot know the beginning phase. An action can become an object of attention only *after* it has occurred. While it is occurring, it cannot be noticed.

To be certain that the reader understands the nature of reflective meaning, we will cite an excerpt from Mead (1956) which demonstrates the same point: "We are conscious always of what we have done, never of doing it. We are always conscious directly only of sensory processes, never of motor processes; hence we are conscious of motor processes only through sensory processes, which are their resultants" (p. 136). Actions are known only when they have been completed.

The next question that must be faced is what to do with the fact that people seem to plan and to guide their actions according to their plans. If everything is retrospective, what are we to do with plans? Schutz's answer to this is imaginative, though difficult to summarize. Basically, his argument is that when one thinks about the future, this thinking is not done in the future tense, but rather in the future perfect tense. If asked what I plan to do, I might say, "I will write a memo to the president requesting a budget increase." Schutz's argument is that what I'm really saying is, "I shall have written a memo to the president requesting a budget increase." I think of the future action as if it had already been completed. My statement contains

---

[4]From A. Schutz, *The Phenomenology of the Social World*, trans. G. Walsh and F. Lehnert (Evanston, Ill.: Northwestern Univ. Press, 1967), p. 51. Reprinted by permission.

both future and past time. Even though a plan appears to be something oriented solely to the future, in fact it also has about it the quality of an act that has already been accomplished. The *meaning* of the actions that are instrumental to the completion of the act can be discovered because they are viewed as if they had already occurred. We have said that meaning is established retrospectively. Thinking in the future perfect tense retains this requirement. The actions gain meaning because attention is directed to them as if they had already occurred.

Note, in addition, that the meaning of the actions is determined by the projected act as a whole (Schutz refers to this as the project). What this means is that the actor visualizes the completed act, not the component actions that will bring about completion. It is only when the realization of this future act is imagined that it is possible for means to be selected. Mead (1956) says the same thing when he remarks, "in general, one sees things which will enable the ongoing activity to be carried out" (p. 137). A similar argument is found in Slack (1955) and in Barnard (1938, p. 36).

To see precisely how Schutz portrays this property of anticipated acts, the reader should study the following quotation:

> [T]he actor projects his action as if it were already over and done with and lying in the past. It is a full-blown, actualized event, which the actor pictures and assigns to its place in the order of experience given to him at the moment of projection. Strangely enough, therefore, because it is pictured as completed, the planned act bears the temporal character of pastness. ... The fact that it is thus pictured as if it were simultaneously past and future can be taken care of by saying that it is thought of in the future perfect tense.[5]

To the original point about retrospective meaning has been added the fact that meanings which seem to be prospective are in fact also retrospective. It becomes apparent also that any action can take on a variety of meanings. The meaning depends on the project in which the action is embedded. But note another crucial variable. The meaning of an action will also change depending on the span of the project. To return to the memo-writing example, the meaning of my making marks on a paper (actions that accomplish the act of getting a budget increase) changes if my project becomes getting a promotion rather than getting a budget increase. It could be that I am trying to increase a budget so that the president will regard me as an ambitious employee who should be promoted. In this case, the meaning of the action of writing changes. Note the problems this creates for the observer who tries to explain whether an actor has reached his goal and, if so, how. The observer's judgment of where an act begins and ends will

---

[5]From A. Schutz, *op. cit.*, p. 61. Reprinted by permission.

always be arbitrary. This could be dubbed the "woodcutter's warning to myopic researchers." "When one is watching a woodcutter it will make a great deal of difference whether we try to analyze 'objectively' the individual blows of the axe or whether we simply ask the man what he is doing and find that he is working for a lumber company" (Schutz, 1967, p. 62).

While we have sketched out some idea of the process by which meaning in general is established, we have yet to indicate how specific meanings arise. The clue to this lies in the nature of the act of attention. Think of the reflective act as a cone of light that spreads backward from a particular present. This light will give definition and contours to portions of lived experience. Since the cone starts in the present, whatever the ego's attitude or mood is at that moment, the identical mood will carry over to the backward glance. The attitude of the ego toward ongoing activity determines its attitude toward the past. Thus, "the *meaning* of a lived experience undergoes modifications depending on the particular kind of attention the Ego gives to that lived experience" (1967, p. 73). The meaning, in other words, is the kind of attention directed to the past. The kind of attention and the meaning of that which is attended to *are one and the same thing.* Since a backward act of attention emanates from a here and now, the attitude that exists in that here and now will determine the kind of attention, which in turn determines what is singled out and given definition. The reader must avoid any tendency to say that meaning is "attached" to the experience that is singled out. This is precisely what meaning is not. Meaning is not something apart from attention, something that exists alongside or above the act of attention for eventual attachment. Instead, the meaning of anything *is* the way it is attended to and nothing else.

To understand this point, one need only assume that the predominant orientation of the human actor is pragmatic (e.g., Mills, 1966; Watzlawick, Beavin, and Jackson, 1967; Schutz, 1967; Mead, 1956). Any here and now may be described as a pragmatic here and now, a here and now in which some projects are visualized, some are underway, and some have just been completed. Any reflective act originates in a here and now where projects are underway and where pragmatic attitudes are uppermost. Since the attitude to life is a pragmatic one, attention is pragmatically conditioned. Whatever items are singled out of the flow of experience for closer attention will take on whatever meaning is implicit in the pragmatic reflective glance. Whatever is now, at the present moment, underway will determine the meaning of everything that has already been accomplished. Meanings, in other words, shift as a function of the projects underway in a here and now. Restated loosely, the present interests of the actor determine the meaning of his lived experiences. A here and now that slips into the past may be attended to or ignored. If attended to, the meaning of that former here and now will be determined by the interests in the immediate here and now. The crucial point is that the meaning is retrospective and is determined by the mode of attention directed to the lived experience.

It is possible to illustrate the preceding points by a phenomenon that Garfinkel (1968) labels "Ed Rose's Function." This phenomenon is based on the following sequence of events. When Ed Rose (a sociologist) visits a strange city and is being driven by his host from the airport to a motel, Rose looks out the car window and at some random moment says, "My, that's changed." In response to this senseless statement, Rose's host usually makes some sensible reply such as "yes, it burned down," "there is some new urban renewal work going on," "the heat plays funny tricks out here," etc. Having heard his host's answer, Rose then is able to discover the meaning of what he said in the first place. Only by hearing the response does Rose discover what the stimulus was. This example illustrates retrospective meaning. Rose refers to something that has already elapsed by the time his host replies. The host is able to make a meaningful statement because he can refer to something that has already occurred, not something that will occur. More importantly, the meaning of Rose's statement resides solely in what the host attends to and singles out of the flow of appearances passing by Rose's window. And this attending itself is pragmatically conditioned. Whatever the host's interests or projects are at that particular moment, they will provide the meaning of that to which the attention is directed. This is so because attention originates in that same here and now where projects are underway. As outside observers, we can't say for certain precisely what project the host was engaged in that led him to single out a site "where something burned down." To speculate about the content of this project in the absence of the host's own report would be to defy the "woodcutter's warning." It is sufficient to state that we would expect to find some linkage between the host's attitude toward the here and now, and the noticing of the burned-out structure.

In this example, Rose could discover what he had said only after he had said it. Even though here a second party provided the backward glance, reflective meaning could just as easily have been provided by the actor himself. Having said, "My, that's changed," Rose could just as easily have sorted back through his own previous knowledge. Whatever he singled out would have been the meaning of his response (e.g., his reflective glance might highlight the item, "Oh, that's the phrase I use whenever I want to play games with my colleagues").

Given this simplified version of only a small portion of Schutz, we have a sufficient number of tools to make more explicit what is meant by an enacted environment. Whenever there are human actors in a collectivity, we can assume that each is immersed in an ongoing flow of experience. Once lived, this experience is *potentially* available for attention, although most of it remains unnoticed. If the actor removes himself from the ongoing stream and gazes reflectively at that which has already passed, then it is possible for his experience to be changed into separable, well-defined experiences, the meaning of which will be determined by whatever his attitude is at that moment toward his ongoing activities. His attitude determines the kind of attention that will be directed backward, and this mode of attention is the meaning that the experiences will have.

We assume that this is the basic manner in which variation occurs within human evolutionary systems. Variation does retain some orderliness. The sequence whereby some portions of the elapsed experience are made meaningful can be viewed as a removing of some of the equivocality that is inherent in a flow of experience. Variation does not produce equivocality; rather, it is the primitive stage at which some equivocality is removed from the ongoing experience—removed by the reflective glance which singles out and defines more sharply some portion or portions of the past experience. *It is these primitive meanings, these bits of enacted information, that constitute the informational input for subsequent processes of selection and retention.* For a human organization, the variation process could be renamed the *enactment* process.

It may appear at first glance that all the equivocality possible is removed in this initial phase, and that there is nothing but unequivocal information passed along to subsequent processes. That this assumption is incorrect can be seen from several vantage points. First, remember that time is continually passing, projects are changing, interests are being modified. Selection occurs in a later here and now than does enactment. A meaning that arises in the enactment phase and seems obvious may become problematic when viewed from a later moment in time. The meaning of the enacted information is not fixed, but fluid. It is fluid precisely because its interpretation varies as a function of the temporal distance from which it is viewed (Schutz, 1967, p. 74). Second, any enacted meaning can exist in one of three forms. The reflective glance can fixate either on the completed deed, on the stages by which the deed was accomplished, or on both (Schutz, 1967, p. 71). This means that the information which is passed along can consist of statements about ends, means, or ends plus means. Since organizational members typically have to justify their actions to supervisors, means plus ends are probably the principal contents that are fed into the selection process. Third, any specific interpretation that emerges from a reflective glance never tells it all. There is always surplus meaning. Portions of the stream of experience which went unnoticed at the moment of the reflective glance can still be noticed on some future occasion. "No lived experience can be exhausted by a single interpretive scheme" (Schutz, 1967, p. 85). Now one may question whether this potential multiplicity of meanings is passed along to the group or retained in the head of the actor who makes the interpretation. After all, it is *his* lived experience, and in this sense it is absolutely private (Bridgman, 1959). But though the lived experience, in all its variety, may not be transmitted at a given moment in time, it still remains to shade the meanings given to all the actor's subsequent experiences; it can be reconstituted and rearranged. Eventually, then, sizable portions of this lived experience probably do get transmitted to the group selection process.

Another crucial point is implied in this discussion. Up until the information reaches the selection process, it is pragmatically conditioned by the interests of the *individual* actor. His interests, and his interests alone, determine the meaning. But when this information is passed along to the selection process, collective rather than individual pragmatics control the establishment of meaning. This being the case, it is likely that different components of the input will be attended to, in different ways, with the eventual establishment of different meanings. Stated in another way, information that is unequivocal for the individual can be equivocal and problematic for the system. The first time the system "intercepts" the individual informational inputs is when the selection process is applied to the input. This should not be read as positing anything like a group mind. Instead, selection consists of criteria built up from collective action, criteria that maintain collective action, and the implications of any given individual input for the functioning of the collective structure necessarily are different than they are for the individual. Selfish acts preserve the individual but destroy the collectivity. The same actions can be more or less equivocal depending on the aggregate level from which they are retrospectively viewed.

From still another standpoint we can see that enactment produces equivocal inputs for selection. While it is true that enactment refers to the constituting of an environment by actors, it also remains true that actors live in situations. These situations are continuously changing even if the actor takes account of them only occasionally. Now it is probable that in human organization the environment impinges on the variation process and *not on the selection process*. Though it is never made explicit in evolutionary theory, if a theorist drew a box labeled "ecological change," and had to connect it to either variation, selection, or retention, he would probably attach it to selection. His argument would be that selection is biased by environmental changes, and it produces the fit of the organism to the environment. But we have already seen (p. 62) that selection and adaptation do *not* seem to fit quite as closely as has been assumed. They are, in fact, separable, as is demonstrated by the phenomenon of superstitious behavior. Our proposal, then, is that ecological change affects actions directly, rather than selection. Its impact on the human organization arises from the control it gains over the actions that are emitted. And it is these actions, under the control of ecological changes, that are the raw material out of which primitive meanings are created and passed along. This means that one determinant of action and meanings in the enactment process is *not* present in the selection process. Since the determinants of the enactment process are thus more diverse than those of the selection process, any output from enactment will be equivocal relative to selection.

As a final point, it has been noted that the selection process is analogous to a decision center in organizations. This means that selection is the hub into which inputs are fed from diverse sets of actors. Enactment as a process is only loosely structured, and this means that the diversity of its outputs can be substantial. It is the function of the selection process to sort these equivocal outputs and make them less equivocal. The enactment process is more concerned with doing and less concerned with questions of "why am I doing this?" or "what are the implications for the system?" These questions are answered in the selection process. In other words, enactment is less constrained than are the other processes. The only major constraint it operates under is that of making interpretable those actions that have already occurred. Remember that we are trying to preserve within the enactment process the basic properties of the variation mechanism in evolutionary theory. The variation mechanism constitutes the prototypic instance which we are trying to refine into something consistent with the properties of human actors. Although we have made it more orderly, our version of the variation process is still a way of producing many diverse variations.

CHAPTER SIX

How Organizing Processes Operate

So far, we have described three organizing processes and some of their properties. Our interest now is in describing the inner workings of these processes. This is the most crucial and also the most complex transition. As we said earlier, any process is able to remove from an input only that amount of equivocality that is present in the process itself. This creates the specific problem that one must postulate how a process can become sufficiently disordered to register the amount of equivocality in the input, and yet retain sufficient order to remove some of the equivocality that it has registered. If a process can only register equivocality, then the process will become more disorderly as the input becomes more equivocal, until the process finally destroys itself in total chaos. But a process geared solely to removing equivocality will also destroy itself, since it will operate on increasingly smaller portions of the informational input and will become more and more isolated from the environment in which it operates.

To handle this dual problem of registration and removal, we can postulate that any process contains two elements, assembly rules and interlocked behavior cycles. Assembly rules are rules for assembling the process out of the total pool of interlocked cycles that are available within the organization. These rules consist of criteria by which some subset of all the possible interlocked behavioral cycles relevant to the process is actually selected for application to the informational input. Some examples of assembly rules are the following:

1. Effort: select those cycles whose completion requires the least effort.

2. Frequency: select those cycles that have occurred most frequently in the past.

3. Success: select those cycles that have been most successful in removing equivocality.

4. Permanence: select those cycles that will produce the most stable change in the input.

5. Duration: select those cycles that can be completed in the shortest period of time.

6. Availability: select those cycles that are not currently engaged in other activities.

7. Personnel: select those cycles that are "manned" by more experienced people.

8. Relevance: select those cycles that most closely resemble the assumed content of the input.

9. Reward: select those cycles that the members regard as most rewarding.

10. Disturbance: select those cycles that will cause the least disruption in the ongoing system.

This list suggests some kinds of rules that might be employed; it is not intended to be exhaustive. The important point at the moment is that we are hypothesizing the existence of rules by which processes are constructed. We assume that there are several such rules, and that each of them contains a criterion for selecting, from the pool of all possible interlocked cycles, the specific subset of cycles which will be applied to the actual informational input.

We now assume that assembly rules are the means by which the degree of equivocality is registered accurately in any process. Specifically, it is assumed that the greater the amount of equivocality present in the input, the *fewer* the number of rules that are activated to compose the process. Conversely, the smaller the amount of equivocality in the input, the greater the number of rules that are used to assemble the process.

One may be tempted to argue that a direct relationship is more plausible. It may appear that the greater the equivocality, the more rules one would need to handle it. To think in this way is to miss the point that registration precedes removal. The registration is accomplished by the assembly rules. If an input is equivocal, there is uncertainty as to exactly what it is and how it is to be handled; this makes it more difficult to judge what the appropriate cycles would be. As a result, only a small number of rather general rules are used to assemble the process. However, if the input is less equivocal, there is more certainty as to what the item is and how it should be handled; hence a greater number of rules can be applied in assembling a process to deal with this input.

Now to understand how equivocality is removed, we must discuss the cycles that are actually selected for inclusion in the process. But before discussing cycle selection, it is important to illustrate what cycles consist of. The following is a hypothetical description of a few cycles that might be appropriate for assembly into a selection process. Each row constitutes a separate cycle.

Act	*Interact*	*Double interact*
Action by Person	Response by Other Person	Readjustment by First Person
1. Isolates a property of the input for closer examination	Accepts or rejects this choice	Abandons, revises, or maintains the property
2. Selects criterion for application to input property	Accepts or rejects criterion	Abandons, revises, or maintains criterion
3. Constructs new selection criterion	Accepts or rejects construction	Abandons, revises, or maintains construction
4. Differentiates an existing criterion, bringing out a new component	Accepts or rejects differentiation	Abandons, revises, or maintains
5. Assembles a set of criteria for application to input	Accepts or rejects assemblage	Abandons, revises, or maintains assemblage
6. Applies assembled criteria to input	Assesses criterion-input fit	Accepts or rejects for retention

These six cycles have the following characteristics. Each consists of a double interact. The person performs some action, which is accepted or modified by a second person, after which the first person makes some response to what the second person did. This is the basic influence sequence proposed by Hollander and Willis (1967) as necessary to distinguish conformity, independence, and anticonformity. In the second and third stages of each cycle there are choice points. For example, in cycle 1 the Other Person can accept or reject the choice of an input property, and after he has done so, the First Person can either accept or reject what the Other has done. Note that since there are two choices within the cycle, the ties among the components of this cycle are variable. It is these variabilities that decrease over time as the cycle occurs repeatedly, and it is in this sense that the cycles become a stable collective structure. If, in the initial execution of cycle 1, the Other Person accepts the designation of a relevant input and the First Person maintains this designation, then the next time this cycle is activated, this same pattern is even more likely to occur. The same intensification is assumed to occur for all of the cycles that are listed. Note also that each cycle is directed toward removing equivocality. Some of the cycles are more directly involved in this removal than others. For example, differentiation of new criteria from an existing criterion (cycle 4) contributes indirectly to removal, whereas the cycle involving the application of criteria to the input (cycle 6) directly involves removal.

Now the selection *process* consists of a set of any two or more of the interlocked cycles. The actual set that constitutes the process at any one time is a function of the number and kind of assembly rules that are applied to the pool of all possible cycles. The relationship between rules and cycles is assumed to be the following. The number of cycles that are selected and applied to an information input depends on the number of assembly rules that are activated. The greater the number of rules used to select the cycles, the smaller the number of cycles that will be selected and applied to the input. Conversely, the fewer the number of rules that are used to select cycles, the greater the number of cycles that will be applied to the input.

This latter point may sound inconsistent with the argument that assembly rules determine the cycles that will be selected. But to think in this way is to miss the nature of assembly rules. If you look back at the rules, you will note that any *one* rule is rather gross. If it were applied to the pool of all possible cycles, it would select a large number of cycles. For example, if the frequency rule alone were used to assemble the process, then all cycles that have occurred frequently in the past would be selected for application. Suppose now that two rules rather than one were employed. Suppose that frequency *and* duration were the rules used to compose the process. Now the frequency rule would select all cycles that had occurred frequently in the past, *but* this population would be further reduced in number because only those cycles which were completed in the shortest possible time would be retained. Thus the actual number of cycles applied to the input would become smaller.

The reader may have trouble visualizing just what the concept "pool of cycles" refers to. The picture which may come to mind is that of endless dyads sitting around the organization, waiting to be plugged into some process, after which they will return to their offices to await new inputs. But the cycles that are referred to here should be understood in the full context of interstructured behaviors. When behaviors are selected for a process, what actually happens is that interpersonal networks are selected. For a single person to do what is asked of him requires that he activate those interactions and collective structures that typically enable him to produce the required act. In other words, the task of managing equivocality requires that stable *interaction* patterns be activated. It is in this sense that we are talking about cycles. Interstructured behaviors are the crucial element of organizing, and the removal of equivocality is predominately an interpersonal activity. (See Newcomb, Turner, and Converse, 1965, for an elaboration of this argument.)

With these tools in hand, we can now describe the stages that occur whenever a process becomes activated. First, the amount of equivocality present in an input determines the number of rules that will be activated to select the cycles which will compose the process. This is the most crucial part of the formulation that is beginning to emerge, and the reader is urged to note this particular stage and what it consists of. We are saying that any input to any process has its initial impact on the *rules* that will be used to assemble the process. When we begin to draw lines *between* processes indicating that one process is related to another process, what those lines will mean is that, whatever effect an earlier process has had on an informational item, when that item is passed along to another process, the amount of equivocality in the item will determine the number of assembly rules that are activated in the second process. The exact relationship between equivocality and the number of rules used to assemble a process is assumed to be an inverse one. The greater the amount of equivocality, the fewer the number of rules; the smaller the amount of equivocality, the greater the number of rules.

The next important relationship is that between the number of rules activated and the number of cycles selected for application to the input. If the number of rules is small, a large number of cycles will fulfill these primitive criteria and will be included in the process. However, as the number of rules increases, the number of cycles that will fit all the rules sharply declines. Stated more precisely, the relationship between number of rules and number of cycles selected is also an inverse relationship.

The third important relationship is that between the number of cycles and the amount of equivocality that can be removed when these cycles are applied to the input. The relationship between cycles and removal of equivocality is assumed to be a *direct* one. The greater the number of cycles applied to the input, the greater the amount of equivocality that is removed. The fewer the number of cycles applied to the input, the smaller the amount of equivocality that is removed. All we are saying here is that, if an equivocal input is handled by a large number of separate cycles, then it is more likely that its equivocality will be removed than if it is handled by a small number of cycles.

The final stage in the cycling of a process concerns the relationship between the amount of equivocality removed and the amount of equivocality remaining in the original input. This relationship is straightforward and is assumed to be an inverse one. The greater the amount of equivocality removed from the input, the smaller the amount of equivocality remaining.

By the addition of this step the process completes itself, becoming a closed loop, and the state of the information at this final stage—whatever it may be—is the state of the information when it is passed along to the next process. When the information reaches this final stage in a process, as much of the equivocality has been removed from it as is possible, given the rules and cycles that were associated with the process at this particular point in time. The degree of equivocality still remaining in the information, once it has passed through all steps of the process, is the degree of equivocality that the subsequent process will have to accommodate to and work on.

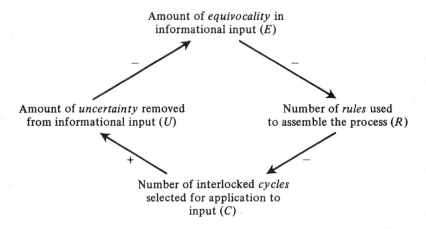

Fig. 2   Sequence of a process.

A graphic presentation of these stages in a process is found in Fig. 2. The notation on the lines connecting the various stages is read as follows: A negative sign indicates an inverse relationship—as one variable increases, the other decreases. A positive sign indicates a direct relationship—as one variable increases, the other also increases.

IMPLICATIONS OF THIS VIEW OF PROCESS

In this section we want to point out some implications of this view of the inner workings of a process, so that the reader can see how some properties found in natural organizations are handled.

It is assumed that all three processes of enactment, selection, and retention unfold in the same sequential manner that has been described. It is obvious, however, that these are different processes, and we may wonder how these differences are preserved if we think of processes in this general way. The differences among the three processes are defined by (1) the kinds of assembly rules that are associated with each, (2) the population of cycles that is regarded as relevant for inclusion in each process, and (3) the amount of equivocality in the typical inputs on which the process operates.

It should be clear, for example, that the inputs to the enactment and selection processes are more equivocal than are those for the retention process. By the time information reaches the retention process, considerable equivocality has already been removed. But we must not overlook some of the more critical properties of the retention process. Even though informational output from the selection process is lower in equivocality than it was at the time it was input, it still remains true that most items have "surplus meaning" and in this sense retain some equivocality. Furthermore, it must be remembered that the retention process has two sources of equivocality with which it must contend, not just one. There is equivocality from the inputs provided by the selection process *and* there is the equivocality that develops from contradictions between newer and older items of retained content. The retention process is the only process in which old information constitutes an "internal" environment which must be contended with.

The reader may be annoyed that specific lists of cycles and rules have not been provided for each of the three processes. One reason is that these lists have to be discovered by observation and empirical research, and there isn't much information about them readily available. But there is a more important point. As one moves from organization to organization, there should be considerable differences in the contents of these rules and cycles. If we specified one set of contents, we would obscure the point that we are trying to develop a way of thinking about organizations *in general*. Our concern is with general properties of organizing, properties that will fit a variety of organizations, and in this sense content is *not* one of our crucial concerns. Whatever organization you choose to observe, there should be three major processes that unfold in the manner described; if you can locate these processes and watch their unfolding, *then* you can determine their specific contents in that particular organization.

The reader may also wonder what happens to routine informational inputs, those inputs that occur over and over again, that are expected and are handled as a matter of course, with little attention paid to their contents because they are so familiar. There seems to be something dreadfully cumbersome about each little item's going through all these complicated steps. First, it should be clear that we *are* saying that every information item, regardless of its clarity or ambiguity, *does* go through all these stages. Second, we should look more closely at what this view predicts in the case of a routine item. If we do this, we will find that routine items are not as simple as we have imagined in the past. If an item is routine, we can reasonably assume that it has a low degree of equivocality. It has some unclarity, but not nearly so much as would a sudden, unexpected, unprecedented input. Now when the unequivocal, routine item intrudes into a process, the following things occur: numerous rules are activated to handle the input, few cycles are assembled into the process, and *little of the equivocality of the input is removed.* This means that most of the equivocality that was in the original input *remains* there. Now, assuming that this is what happens at each stage, note that when this routine item eventually gets to the retention process, it still has some, though not much, equivocality. Now if there were a great amount of equivocality still left by this stage, there would be a lot for the retention process to do (few rules, many cycles, much equivocality removed); since all this work would be done amidst the prior experience already embedded in the retention process, the chances are that in the end the new item would be fitted very closely to the old retained content. But when considerable equivocality has been removed from an item *prior* to its reaching the retention process—as is the case with a routine item—there is little that the retention process can do with this item (low equivocality, many rules, few cycles, little removal), and this could mean that it is *hard* to assimilate the item into past experience. The interesting thing about this entire sequence is that routine items are difficult to revise. Whatever equivocality resides in them is in a sense sealed off from any further work by the processes. For this reason, they can cause more trouble than more equivocal items.

With the concepts we now have in hand, it is also possible to talk more concretely about choice points in organizing. Earlier it was noted that there are two choices—one regarding selection and one regarding enactment—and that these choices are under the control of the retention process. The exact nature of these choices can now be made more explicit. They are concerned with whether the human actor treats retained information as equivocal information or unequivocal information. Typically, the information in the retention process, once it has been filtered by the two earlier processes of enactment and selection, is unequivocal information. But the human actor has the choice of whether he wants to treat this information as equivocal or unequivocal when he is making decisions about how he will act and choose in the future. Earlier we said that whenever a person decides to act or choose in a manner different from the way he has in the past, he is discrediting some portion of his past experience. We can now update this discussion and say that when a person discredits retained content, what he does is ascribe to that retained content an amount of equivocality *opposite* to what it had after passing through the organizing processes. If the retained content is unequivocal, then the actor discredits it by treating it as equivocal. If the retained content is equivocal, the actor treats it as unequivocal. On the other hand, when the actor decides to act or choose on the basis of retained content, and decides *not* to discredit it in his future acts and choices, then he ascribes to the retained content the *same* amount of equivocality that it has in the retention process. It should not be assumed that we are talking about processes of distortion, fantasy, or irrationality. Instead, we are asserting that retained content, even though it is relatively unequiv-

CHAPTER SEVEN

How Organizing Processes
Are Interconnected

The concepts presented so far refer to the elements that go into a process, the nature of the processes themselves, the ways in which processes adapt to the state of their informational inputs, and the principles by which separate processes function. What has not been discussed is the ways in which the processes are interconnected. This chapter is devoted to the topic of relationships among processes.

It will be recalled that the relationships that exist among processes *are* the controls of the system (see p. 37). The relationships are assumed to be ones of mutual causation. This means that the amount of influence which variable X exerts over variable Y determines the amount Y exerts over X; and the influence of Y over X then determines the subsequent influence of X over Y. For example, the greater the amount of oppression by authorities, the greater the amount of rebellion by subordinates; and the greater the rebellion, the greater the amount of subsequent oppression. This mutually causal relationship is to be distinguished from the situation in which the size of influence in one direction is independent of the size in the opposite direction, and the situation in which the size of influence in both directions is caused by some third factor.

Causal or control relationships can be of two kinds. They can be either direct (+) or inverse (−). If there is a direct causal relationship from one variable to another, changes will occur in the *same* direction. If there is an increase in one variable, there will be an increase in the other variable; and if there is a decrease in one variable, there will be a decrease in the other. The reader must be careful to note that a direct causal relationship can involve either increases or decreases. An inverse, or negative, causal relationship is present when one variable changes in one direction and another variable changes in the *opposite* direction. For example, if one process increases in the speed with which it is executed, the other process will decrease in speed. Or if one process decreases in speed, the other process will increase in speed.

Any system consists of several causal relationships, some direct and some inverse. The crucial factor about these relationships is that their pattern determines the fate of the system. The system is not controlled by any single relationship. To understand the system, we must know *all* the causal relationships and whether they are direct or inverse; we must determine the consequences of the entire pattern of relationships.

Fortunately, it is possible to get some leverage on this difficult problem with the work of Maruyama (1963). The nature of his approach can be illustrated by the causal network portrayed in Fig. 3.[1] The several processes in this figure are connected by either positive or negative lines. For example, the positive line between P and G signifies that the greater the number of people in a city, the greater the amount of garbage that will be produced per area; and the fewer the number of people in a city, the smaller the amount of garbage per area. The negative line from sanitation facilities (S) to number of diseases (D) means that the greater the number of sanitation facilities, the *fewer* the number of diseases; and the fewer the number of sanitation facilities, the *greater* the number of diseases.

In this figure certain sets of processes form cycles or closed loops. There is a loop from P to M to C and back to $P;$ there is another loop from P to M to S to D and back to $P;$ and there are more loops which the reader can identify for himself. Each loop has a pattern of direct and inverse relationships; one way of describing this pattern is to count the number of inverse relationships. Any loop contains either an even or an odd number of negative signs. And herein lies the crucial property of any set of causal relationships within a system. A loop that contains an odd number of negative signs is self-correcting—that is, it is able to counteract any deviations that may appear. But any loop that contains an even number of negative signs is not self-correcting, and any deviations in it will be amplified unchecked.

To illustrate these two principles, we can examine specific loops in Fig. 3. The *PMCP* loop has an even number of negative signs (zero); therefore it should be deviation-amplifying and should eventually destroy itself. If we trace the relationships, we will discover that this is precisely the case. If the number of people in a city increases, there will be an increase in modernization, which in turn will cause more people to migrate to the city; this increased migration will further increase the number in the city; the further

---

[1]Fig. 3 is reprinted by permission from M. Maruyama, "The Second Cybernetics: Deviation-Amplifying Causal Processes," *American Scientist, 51* (1963), pp. 164-179.

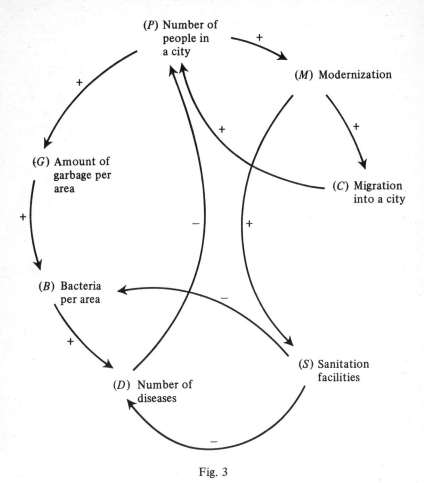

Fig. 3

increase in number will further increase modernization; etc. There is no check on the number of people that come into the city; once the number increases the process will continue unchecked until the system breaks down. This same consequence occurs no matter where we start the loop. Rather than starting it at the number of people in the city, we could just as easily start it at modernization, with the same results. As modernization increases, there is greater migration, more people, more modernization, more migration, etc.

To get an even better idea of how a loop with an even number of negative causal relationships can self-destruct, consider the loop which consists of *PMSDP*. This loop has two negative relationships—again an even number. Negative relationships ordinarily are capable of controlling the system, because they can reverse the effects of an earlier variable; but when there is an even number of negative relationships, this capability for reversing earlier effects is *canceled.* To illustrate, suppose that the number of people in the city increases. There will be more modernization, an increase in sanitation facilities, a *decrease* in diseases, and then a further *increase* in the number of people. Since the two negative relationships cancel each other out, there is no control over the number of people in the city. The number will increase indefinitely until the system breaks down. It could break down, for instance, because modernization could no longer be increased, sanitation facilities could not be expanded, etc.

To see how an odd number of negative relationships can counteract deviation and produce control, examine the loop *PGBDP.* This loop contains one negative relationship. As the number of people increases, garbage increases, bacteria increase, diseases increase, and then the number of people in the city *decreases.* To continue, as the number of people in the city decreases, there will be a decrease in garbage, bacteria, and diseases, which will then cause an *increase* in the number of people. In other words, the number of people in the city is held stable around some number. Any temporary increase or decrease in population is counteracted by the cycle's single, uncanceled, negative relationship.

Now if we put all the various loops together, and consider the whole of Fig. 3 as one system, we can ask what the fate of the system will be. Some loops suggest that the system will destroy itself, but others suggest that it will maintain a controlled existence. There are two ways in which we might handle this problem of predicting the fate of a system containing several closed loops. First, we could assume that the loops are of *unequal* importance. If we make this assumption, we would scale the different loops on their degrees of importance, and we would predict that the fate of the system would be determined by the nature of its most important loop. If the most important loop is deviation-counteracting, then the *system* in which that loop is embedded will be deviation-counteracting. If the most important loop is deviation-amplifying, then the system will be deviation-amplifying. The difficulty with this method of predicting is that the judgment of a loop's importance may often be purely arbitrary. However, there are some ways in which this problem of arbitrariness can be solved. It is possible, for example, to define importance in terms of the number of inputs to and outputs from the different elements in the system. The general rule would be: the greater the number of inputs to and/or outputs from an element, the more important that element is. Having assessed the individual elements, we would then search for that loop which contained the greatest number of important elements, and we would predict that the nature of that loop would determine the fate of the system. For example, if we examine the elements in Fig. 3, we find that some of them have more than one output (this is true of elements *P, M,* and *S*) and some of them have more than one input (this is true of elements *P, D,* and *B*). Now if we assume that the five elements with more than one output or more than one input are the most important elements in the system, then we look for that closed loop within this system which contains the greatest number of these important elements. We discover that there is a loop that contains all five elements (the loop goes from P to M to S to B to D to P). Since this loop has an even number of negative signs (two), it is deviation-amplifying. Thus we say that the most important loop within this system is deviation-amplifying, and therefore the entire system is deviation-amplifying; we predict that it will eventually destroy itself unless one of the relationships changes in sign, another relationship is added, or some relationship is deleted.

All this pertains to the situation in which the investigator assumes that the loops are of unequal importance. If we make the assumption that the loops are of *equal* importance, then we can solve the problem of predicting the fate of a system in a different way. It seems plausible that we could talk about the fate of the system *as a system* by counting the number of negative *cycles,* just as we previously counted the number of negative relationships. By a "negative cycle" we mean a closed loop that contains an odd number of negative causal relationships. We would predict that any system will survive as a system only if it contains an odd number of these negative cycles. If the system contains an even number of negative cycles, then their effects will cancel one another and the remaining positive cycles will amplify whatever deviations may occur. Another way of reaching the same prediction would be to count the total number of negative relationships in the whole system, counting each negative more than once if it appeared in more than one cycle. If the total number was odd, the system would be deviation-counteracting; if it was even, the system would be deviation-amplifying.

Now we can refer back to Fig. 3. In this figure *one* of the four cycles is negative (the *PGBDP* cycle), and there is a total of five negative causal relationships (counting the one between D and P three times, since it takes part in three cycles). Since both these numbers are odd, whatever happens within this system, regardless of where it happens, will eventually be reversed. The system, according to this prediction, is a deviation-counteracting system. This prediction, however, appears to contradict our earlier prediction based on the assumption that the loops were of unequal strength. Using that assumption, we predicted that the system would eventually disintegrate. But if we refine our second analysis, the analysis based on equal strength, we can remove some of this apparent contradiction. Make the following assumptions:

1.   Assume that there is a sudden influx of 5000 new people into a city that has a stable population of 20,000.

2.   Assume that each loop controls 2000 people. If the loop is deviation-amplifying, at the completion of each cycle it will have added 2000 people to the population; if it is deviation-counteracting, it will have subtracted 2000 people from the population.

3.   Assume that each loop takes the same amount of clock time to complete its cycle.

With these assumptions and hypothetical numbers, it is now possible to see what happens within this system as a consequence of the influx of 5000 people. At the time the system is activated, the population is 25,000. When the *PMCP* loop completes its course, 2000 people will be added to this figure; 2000 more will be added by the *PMSDP* loop, and 2000 more by the *PMSBDP* loop. The *PGBDP* loop will remove 2000 people. Thus at the completion of the first cycle within this system, there will be 29,000 people. There has been some control exerted by the one deviation-counteracting loop, but this control is relatively slight when compared with the three other deviation-amplifying loops. The system is steadily increasing in size; its growth is only moderately controlled. The same gradual escalation would be found even if we dropped the assumption of equal clock time for cycle completion. In this way we can bring our prediction based on loops of equal strength into line with our previous prediction based on loops of unequal strength.

To make the transition from this general way of thinking about relationships among processes to the specific problem of explaining how organizing occurs, it is important to note that *both* deviation-amplifying and deviation-counteracting loops are necessary for a system. The deviation-amplifying loops provide the means whereby a system can change its condition, elaborate its structure, or generate patterns of responding that it has not generated before. Deviation-counteracting loops are the means whereby systems maintain stability and continuity; they are the self-correcting control loops that enable the organization to preserve and act upon the "lessons" it has learned from experience.

If the reader now reexamines Fig. 2 (p. 77), in which the stages in a process were described, he will discover that individual processes are deviation-counteracting. A process, as a process, should be capable of handling whatever inputs it receives and still remain intact. This basic intactness of the processes involved in organizing is one of the reasons why it is important to take processes seriously when we think about organizations. Processes have a degree of durability, resilience, and self-control which suggests that they should be prominent within organizations.

The specific problem we face at this point is specifying how the several processes involved in organizing are related. The intent of this chapter has been to develop some basic notions about relationships among processes so that we could apply these ideas to the concrete problem of determining the relationships among enactment, selection, and retention. Before we get into this problem, we will summarize the relevant notions that have been developed up to this point. We have argued that (1) there are three organizing processes—enactment, selection, and retention; (2) these processes are linked together such that retention affects both selection and enactment;

(3) organizing among humans involves two choice points, the choice regarding how to act and the choice regarding what to select; and (4) the external environment in the form of ecological change impinges on the enactment process rather than on the selection process. We can depict these relationships graphically as follows:

Ecological change $\longrightarrow$ Enactment $\longrightarrow$ Selection $\longrightarrow$ Retention

It is now possible to bring in some notions that have been lurking in earlier chapters. First, it should be noted that the lines leading from one process to another are information lines. They represent the transmission of information from one process to another process. Second, it will be recalled that information is equivocal, and it is the work of the processes to remove some of this equivocality. Thus the lines leading from one process to another do not refer simply to information: they refer to information that contains varying degrees of equivocality. Third, it will be recalled that in order to remove equivocality from an input, a process must first register the degree of equivocality in that input.

We have shown that equivocality is registered by the increase or decrease in the number of rules that are activated to assemble a process. And the number of rules in turn affects the entire way in which that process is assembled and applied, and what the condition of the information will be once the steps in the process have been completed. If we label a process in which few rules are activated an *equivocal process,* and a process in which numerous assembly rules are activated an *unequivocal process,* then we can specify the nature of the causal relationships in the preceding diagram. The amount of equivocality in an informational input determines the degree of equivocality of a process. If information is high in equivocality, few rules will be activated to assemble a process, and the process will therefore be equivocal. If information is low in equivocality, many rules will be activated to assemble a process, and the process will be unequivocal. What we have, then, is a direct relationship between information and processes. The more equivocal the input, the more equivocal the process. The following diagram represents a more complete portrait of what we are proposing:

Ecological change $\xrightarrow{+}$ Enactment $\xrightarrow{+}$ Selection $\xrightarrow{+}$ Retention

$(+, -)$

$(+, -)$

The $(+, -)$ designation on the two lines leading from retention to selection and from retention to enactment indicates that the actor has the choice of whether the causal relationship will be direct or inverse. As we noted earlier, the actor can choose how to use his retained content. He can either credit this content and use it as a prescriptive guide for subsequent actions or choices, or he can discredit it. If he chooses to regard retained information as prescriptive, he will use this information as a direct guide in activating the assembly rules for his subsequent choices or behavior. These future assembly rules will be under the direct control of the amount of equivocality found in the retained content. If that retained content is equivocal, then his subsequent activation of either the selection process (choice) or enactment process (act) will be equivocal—that is, he will use *few* rules to assemble the process. If the retained content is unequivocal, then his subsequent activation of either the selection process or the enactment process will be unequivocal—that is, he will use *many* rules in assembling the process. Either of these outcomes is possible if the retained content is treated as prescriptive and is implemented on subsequent occasions.

But if the actor discredits retained content, he will assemble the subsequent selection or enactment process in a manner which is *contrary to* the amount of equivocality present in the retained content. If the retained content is equivocal, he will activate a *large* number of assembly rules; if the retained content is unequivocal, he will activate a *small* number of assembly rules. In terms of Fig. 2, what we are arguing is that when an actor discredits retained content, he changes the normal inverse relationship $(-)$ between E and R to a direct $(+)$ relationship. The important feature of this reversal is that the actor assembles the process in such a way that new inputs are generated and fed into the system.

To see how this works, assume that retained content is unequivocal and that the actor decides to discredit this information in the enactment process. Normally, when unequivocal retained content is fed back into the enactment process, a number of rules are activated for application to this content. But when the decision to discredit is made, fewer assembly rules are activated. This means that more cycles will be activated, and that more equivocality will be removed from that unequivocal input. But how could more equivocality be removed when there was very little there in the first place? The answer is simple. Even though the content is unequivocal, it can be reinterpreted in a number of different ways. This was the major point in the earlier discussion of retrospective meaning. Once an item is past history, it can be viewed retrospectively and it can take on a variety of meanings depending on the projects that are underway at the time. Now when assembly rules are reduced in number, and a greater variety of cycles is applied to the unequivocal input, a greater range of implications and meanings will be extracted from the item. What actually happens is that a supposedly unequivocal item is made *more* equivocal. It is in this sense that the decision to discredit past wisdom serves to introduce novelty into a system. Novelty is introduced because the item is rendered more equivocal than it was when it first reached the retention process; out of this newly "discovered" equivocality come new meanings for the item.

In other words, a decision to *discredit* past wisdom is equivalent to establishing an *inverse causal relationship* between retention and one of the two processes with which it is connected. A decision to *credit* past wisdom and to treat it as prescriptive is equivalent to establishing a *direct causal relationship* between retention and one of the two processes with which it is connected. It has been hinted earlier that only if the actor makes dissimilar decisions with respect to his two choices will the system survive. The reason for this argument can now be understood in terms of the ideas about deviation-amplification and deviation-counteraction developed in this chapter. If the actor makes dissimilar choices (i.e., one of the lines has a + and the other a −), then the system will be characterized by a positive loop (an even number of negatives) and a negative loop (an odd number of negatives). The system will have an odd number of negative cycles (one in this case) and also an odd number of negative relationships (one in this case, counting both possible loops). If the processes are related in this way, an optimal blend between stability and flexibility is achieved. One process preserves the degree of unequivocality already achieved by the information in the retention system, and the other process generates new implications for the unequivocal content.

CHAPTER EIGHT

A Model for the Study of Organizing

The purpose of this chapter is to pull together the concepts we have suggested as possible ways to solve some of the problems mentioned in Chapter Two. It is important to remember that the intent of this entire book has been to facilitate learning rather than to instruct. This is mentioned simply to specify the manner in which the present model is to be regarded. Our intent is to sensitize the reader to features of organizations that need to be observed more closely and to provide some labels by which he can manipulate and manage the observations that he makes. The concepts that we have used are essentially economizing devices that will enable the reader to store economically a considerable amount of information about organizations.

REVIEW OF BASIC FEATURES OF ORGANIZING

The preceding discussions suggest that an organization can be defined in terms of processes of organizing. The central argument is that any organization *is* the way it runs through the processes of organizing. These processes, which consist of interlocked behaviors, are related and form a system. The relationships of mutual causation that make the separate processes into a system constitute the controls of the system. This means that, depending on the pattern of relationships that exists among the processes, there will be either control or chaos. It must be remembered that it is relationships rather than processes that control the fate of any system. If we take these properties as basic features found in any organization of any size doing any thing, then it is possible to state a formal definition of organization. Organization is fluid, continually changing, continually in need of reaccomplishment, and it appears to be an entity only when this fluidity is "frozen" at some moment in time. This means that we must define organization in terms of organizing. *Organizing consists of the resolving of equivocality in an enacted environment by means of interlocked behaviors embedded in conditionally related processes.*

To summarize these components in a less terse manner, organizing is directed toward information processing in general, and more specifically, toward removing equivocality from informational inputs. This resolution is a two-stage procedure, the execution of which requires that equivocality be first registered and then removed. In order for equivocality to be registered, the order within the process to which the information is an input must match the degree of order in the input. In order for equivocality to be removed, the orderliness within the process must be greater than that in the input. These seemingly incompatible demands are accommodated within the process by the number of cycles applied to the input (these remove equivocality) and the number of assembly rules used to compose the process (these register equivocality).

The informational environment on which processes operate is an enacted environment that is based on retrospective interpretations of actions already completed. These actions are partially under the control of past knowledge and partially under the control of external events. However, only those portions of the environment exist which are constituted by the individual through retrospective attentional processes. It is in this sense that members of organizations actually create the environment to which they then adapt. It is actors and actors alone who separate out for closer attention portions of an ongoing flow of experience. It is their making of experience into discrete experiences that produces the raw material for organizing. This raw material varies in equivocality, but typically has more of it than can be tolerated by the system.

Interlocked behaviors are the basic elements that constitute any organization. They consist of repetitive, reciprocal, contingent behaviors that develop and are maintained between two or more actors. Each actor uses and is used by the other person for the accomplishment of activities which neither alone could accomplish. The resolving of equivocality is assumed to be a joint activity, an activity that is accomplished by sets of actors who interlock varying sets of behaviors. Each interlocked behavioral cycle can remove some equivocality, but it is only when several different cycles are applied to the information that a sufficient degree of certainty is produced for unequivocal action to be taken.

These interlocked behavioral cycles are embedded in three separate processes. The enactment process creates the information that the system adapts to, and in doing so removes a small amount of equivocality. However, the amount removed is substantially less than is removed by the processes of selection and retention. The greatest share of equivocality is removed by the selection process. On the basis of criteria established by past experience, the selection process sorts through the variety present in the equivocal information, admits those portions which satisfy the criteria, and thereby puts the equivocal information into orderly form. The final process is retention. Although this process is basically a storage process, it also removes some equivocality by integrating newer items with items previously retained. Any information passed along from the selection process has the potential to contradict or reaffirm preexisting content. Internal reorganization of information within the retention system removes the equivocality produced by contradictions.

These three processes are interrelated and they constitute a system. The basic relationships among the processes are control relationships. They represent the ways in which processes are determined by the state of their informational inputs. In general, these relationships are direct causal linkages. This means that the same degree of equivocality will be created in the process as exists in its informational input. When there is high equivocality, the rules for composing the process decrease in number; when there is low equivocality, the rules increase in number. The rules, in turn, determine the number of interlocked behavioral cycles that will be assembled for the actual removal of equivocality. The fewer the rules, the greater the number of cycles that are selected.

Though the causal relationships among processes are usually direct, there are two exceptions. The relationships from retention to selection and from retention to enactment are under the control of the actors in the system. These relationships can be made either direct or inverse. Whenever the actor asks what he should do on the basis of what he knows, what he is actually asking is whether he should continue to be guided by the *state* of information in retention or whether he should counteract this state. It was argued that for the system to maintain a balance between stability and flexibility the actor must decide both to preserve and to counteract what he already knows. He does this by binding either selection or enactment directly to the state of information in the retention process and by binding the remaining process inversely to the state of information in the retention process. He maintains both control and variety if he splits his decisions in this way. Past wisdom is preserved, but sufficient flexibility is retained to generate and incorporate new inputs. If the system functions in this way, there is both deviation-amplification and deviation-counteraction. And the system, as a system, will be preserved because it remains basically deviation-counteracting (i.e., it retains an odd number of deviation-counteracting cycles).

The preceding points are summarized graphically in Fig. 4. In this figure we have depicted the hypothesized relationships within a process as well as between processes. The arrows that extend *between* processes signify that the degree of equivocality at the "blunt" end of the arrow determines the

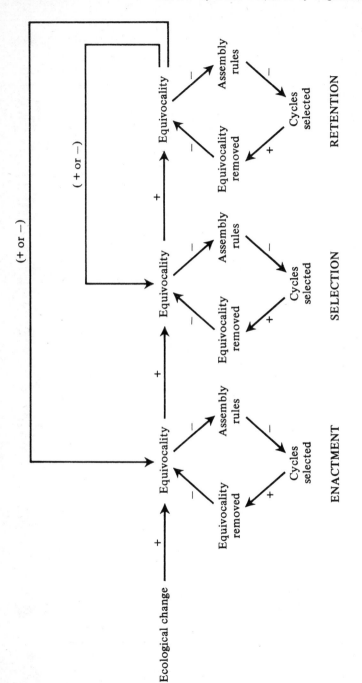

Fig. 4   The organizing model.

degree of equivocality that will be present as input to the process at the "sharp" end of the arrow. These relationships are normally direct, except in the cases of retention to selection and retention to enactment. In these two cases, the relationships can be either direct or inverse, depending on the decisions of the actors in the system.

To illustrate how to read this figure, we will trace through one entire sequence. Assume that there is a high amount of equivocality produced by a sudden ecological change, and that this equivocality is the main input to the enactment process. The high equivocality in the input leads to a small number of assembly rules being activated, a large number of cycles, a relatively large amount of equivocality being removed, and therefore a lesser amount of equivocality present in the input when it reaches the selection process. But when the input reaches the selection process it still has considerable equivocality, so few assembly rules will be activated, many cycles selected, and more equivocality removed, leaving less equivocality in the original input. Now if we assume that most of the equivocality in the input has been removed by now (mainly by the selection process), when the input reaches the retention process there will be *several* rules activated, *few* cycles selected, and *little* equivocality removed. Of the small amount of equivocality that the item originally had when it reached the retention process, most is retained.

Once the input resides in the retention process, it is then fed back in some form to both the selection and enactment processes. It is fed back either as an equivocal input or as an unequivocal input. If it is fed back into the system as an equivocal input, an *inverse* causal relationship is imposed on one or both of the lines leading from retention. Let us assume that the actor decides to impose an inverse causal relationship on the line leading from retention to enactment. What this means is that he treats the unequivocal retained item as if it were *equivocal* for future actions; in other words, he decides to construe it in a wider variety of ways. He activates *few* assembly rules to deal with the item; many cycles are selected and applied to the item; and, finally, a lot of the item's new equivocality is removed. Let us further assume that the actor imposes a direct causal relationship on the line leading from retention to selection. What this means is that he treats the unequivocal retained item as if it were *unequivocal* for future choices; he activates many rules, assembles few cycles, and removes little equivocality, leaving the item practically unchanged.

With this overview in mind, we can comment on a few specific points that may be difficult to grasp. We have spoken about future choices and actions being influenced, but the reader may have trouble deciding where choice and action fit in. The actions are associated with enactment, and the choices are associated with selection; both reside in the *cycles* that are selected. It will be recalled that cycles consist of interstructured *behaviors*. In the case of enactment, the cycles appropriate to this process are concerned with doing, acting, performing. In the case of selection, the appropriate cycles are concerned with choosing which of the prior actions should be repeated, acknowledged, and given the stature of beneficial experience. If the reader will look back at the sample list of cycles associated with the selection process (p. 74), he will see that all of these cycles concern some aspect of choice behavior. The choices produced by the selection process operate on the environment that is produced by the enactment process. And it is clear from the diagram that there are two kinds of input to the enactment process out of which this environment is formed: inputs from *inside* the system (the line from retention to enactment) and inputs from *outside* the system (the line from ecological change to enactment).

This model, as described here, is content-free. This way of presenting the model is intentional. It is assumed that the unique properties of any given organization can be inserted into the model as cycles or assembly rules. The specific properties included in the cycles would be the specific interstructured behaviors and choices that are found in the organization. The assembly rules would be the criteria used in the organization to compose coherent sets of cycles for application to the informational inputs received by and created within that organization.

USING THE MODEL

An obvious question at this point is, "What is one supposed to do with the model?" It is an abstraction that preserves in economical form most of the points that have been developed. In this sense it could be viewed simply as a "reminder" of the basic arguments in the book. But the model also serves as a guide for people who want to watch organizations. The model suggests that if you can obtain two separate items of information about an organization, you should be able to predict what will happen in that organization. The two items that are crucial are (1) the degree of equivocality associated with some significant informational input that is received by some process, and (2) the use that is made of retained content. If you obtain information about the degree of equivocality in some important input, then you can predict the number of rules that will be activated, the number of cycles that will be selected, the amount of equivocality that will be removed, the nature of the input to a subsequent process, and the fate of that informational input as it is processed by the subsequent process. If you obtain information about how retained content is used, then you can specify the nature of the causal relationships from retention to selection and from retention to enactment; you can predict how these two processes of enactment and selection will unfold in the future; and you can predict whether the system in which these processes are embedded will maintain a controlled existence or will show signs of disintegration. If you see that both processes have the same causal relationship to retention (i.e., both lines are plus or both lines are minus), then you would predict that productivity would decrease, absenteeism would increase, turnover would increase, morale would decrease, etc. Each of these latter items is assumed to be an indicator of disintegration.

Now, obviously, understanding an organization is not that simple. We are simply illustrating that the model does direct one's attention to certain organizational properties which might ordinarily seem trivial. In this sense, the model is valuable mainly because it helps us to launch our thinking about organizations and to predict something about what we should see.

While this may sound gratuitous, it is important to emphasize that there is a great deal of work which this model leaves up to the observer. Because of its level of abstraction, it can potentially be applied to units of all kinds, but important details will vary depending on the unit selected. For example, we have talked about processes rather than departments or people. The three processes could all be performed by a dyad; each process could be performed by a separate department; or all could be performed in each department. The specific distribution pattern of processes undoubtedly will affect the way the system operates. However, the basic point here is that once the particular pattern of relationships is specified, predictable consequences should be observed. Even more important, once the observer specifies the elements and relationships, he can test, refine, and even refute the ideas mentioned here. Even though the model is general, it still is refutable. If a system with an odd number of negative cycles disintegrates, or if a system with an even number of negative cycles survives, then we are wrong. If the relationships not under the control of human actors (i.e., enactment $\xrightarrow{+}$ selection $\xrightarrow{+}$ retention) do not exhibit direct causal ties, then we are wrong. And if any of the other assumed causal relationships are nonexistent, then we are wrong. The fact that the model may contain error is relatively unimportant. What is much more important is that if the model is applied and found to be incorrect, the precise things that the observer is looking at probably *are* important for understanding organizations. When he discovers that the model is wrong, he is also likely to discover something that is "right." The model can potentially lead him into interesting territory, territory that is not given much attention in existing theories of organization.

CHAPTER NINE

Implications of
the Organizing Model

We have already discussed some of the organizing model's implications for research. The main drawback of the model as a format for research is that it is abstract; the researcher himself must specify a large number of elements. The model is concerned with relationships, with "pure" organizing. It is content-free, because we assume that content is the medium in which organizing occurs and therefore is of secondary importance. Presumably, the researcher can plug any content he wants to into the model. Once he has done this, he should find the contents undergoing specific changes over time; he should know where to look for these changes and what they should look like. If he finds that unexpected changes occur, then the model is incorrect. But it must be made clear that we are concerned with articulating ideas about organizing in a literal sense. The model is a model of how things relate and what the consequences of this relating are.

Embedded in the model are additional implications. These pertain to existing concepts about organizations and managerial practice. This chapter mentions a few of these implications to help the reader place the model into the context of existing work.

RELATION TO EXISTING CONCEPTS

In this section several concepts commonly discussed in organization theories will be mentioned, and their relevance for the model will be noted. The discussion is selective rather than comprehensive. The purpose is to give the reader some idea of the way in which traditional thinking about organizations is recast by the notions we have presented.

Studies of Communication Networks

The laboratory experiments most often cited as a point of departure for theories of organization are studies involving communication networks (e.g., Faucheux and Mackenzie, 1966; McLachlan, 1961; Shaw, 1964). These studies are cited so often because they include several properties assumed to characterize organizations, properties such as mediated interaction, structure, chain of command, superior-subordinate role relationships, etc.

Viewed in terms of organizing, network studies take on a different set of relevancies. The network studies are of interest partly because they contain situations with interlocked behaviors, and they allow one to watch the development and maintenance of these behaviors. Even though most networks contain more than two people and more than a single relationship, in actual functioning only one dyad and one relationship are activated at any moment in time. The basic unit in the network remains a dyad, the members of which interlock their behaviors relative to the particular components of the task that each possesses. It is also relevant that these dyads are unstable, a point made earlier in the discussion of the minimal social situation (see p. 49). Shaw's (1964) review of network research makes it clear that under some conditions individual needs are asserted to the relative neglect of the relationship. This illustrates the point made several times that within any group there is a basic ambivalence on the part of the members: they tend toward both individual and collective action. Network studies are also relevant because they exhibit the property of partial inclusion (see p. 30 f.). It is selected behaviors, not whole people, that are crucial in the operation of a network.

Another property of networks is that they constitute a form of selection criterion. This point is mentioned by Campbell (1965b) and is supported in recent network studies by Mackenzie (1967). The basic findings are that centralized organizational arrangements seem to be preferred, that they are evolved from quite different starting points, and once evolved they are remarkably persistent. As Campbell states,

> The work of Bavelas, Leavitt, Guetzkow and others [see Guetzkow, 1961] has made it seem likely that a social division of labor or differentiation of roles to provide a single coordinator or communications clearing-house has adaptive value. ... Were this pattern to be found to have general superiority in the coordination of information on the part of aggregates of persons, then the variation-and-selective-retention system would explain the ubiquitous presence of headship institutions, in groups capable of collective action, in indigenous cultures the world over.[1]

---

[1]From D. T. Campbell, "Variation and Selective Retention in Socio-cultural Evolution." In H. R. Barringer, G. I. Blanksten, and R. Mack (Eds.), *Social Change in Developing Areas* (Cambridge, Mass.: Schenkman, 1965). Quote is reprinted by permission from p. 29.

The network research also is of interest because it is possible that the type of network in which members operate could influence the choices they will make about what to do with retained content. It is possible that some forms of network lend themselves more readily than others to the split decision that we have argued must occur if the system is to survive.

Productivity and Satisfaction

Virtually all theories of organization make some statements about the relationship between productivity and satisfaction. Most of these discussions adopt some form of instrumental model. Some theories argue that productivity is instrumental to satisfaction: the more productive the individual, the more satisfied he will be. Others reverse the relationship: the greater the satisfaction, the higher the productivity. Still others argue that productivity will be high if it is seen by the actor as instrumental to the attainment of outcomes that he desires.

An assumption implicit in our preceding analysis is that satisfaction may be tied closely to the removal of equivocality. The greater the clarification of equivocal content, the greater the satisfaction. If we view this as a possible relationship, then it could be argued that productivity still has instrumental relevance, but of a rather special kind. Productivity will be high only if it is regarded as a means for removing equivocality. If the actor does not think that high productivity will resolve the equivocality in the informational inputs for which he is responsible, then he will expend a minimally acceptable amount of effort. With minimal effort expenditure and minimal removal of equivocality, satisfaction should also be low.

What we are proposing is that satisfaction is determined by the extent to which an actor can remove equivocality from his environment. In this sense, we are arguing that satisfaction is tied to something like an effectance motive (White, 1959). Byrne and Clore (1967) describe this motive in the following way: "any situation which provides evidence of one's predictive accuracy, ability to understand, correctness, logicality, reality orientation, behavioral appropriateness—any information which permits or indicates effective functioning—would satisfy the effectance motive" (p. 4). Successful removal of equivocality will be rewarding, and the actor's satisfaction will be reflected in his self-reports. Whatever actions contribute to this successful removal will be reinforced, and will be more likely to be repeated on subsequent occasions. Thus, if the actor's performance of an assigned task removes equivocality in the informational inputs he attends to, then productivity and satisfaction should become more closely tied together, and both should be high.

It is interesting, given this analysis, to reexamine the venerable problem of the assembly-line worker (Friedmann, 1954; Walker and Guest, 1952), who contributes a very small portion of a finished product and does this operation repeatedly. A common assertion is that the assembly-line worker is typically dissatisfied because demands on his skills are slight and because he seldom is able to see the relevance of his contribution to the finished product. We can analyze this situation within the present model. The assembly-line worker is one whose task performance removes very little equivocality from his informational input. If he puts three bolts into each automobile frame that passes him, we could say that when the frame reaches him it is in a state of high equivocality (it can become any one of a number of things), and that his efforts remove virtually none of this equivocality. The information leaves him in almost the same condition as when he received it; the frame, when it contains his three bolts, still could become a car, truck, or junk. Note also that this is an instance in which the equivocality in the process does *not* match the equivocality of the input. There is an inverse relationship between the state of information in the input and the state of the process applied to the input. The car frame is equivocal, bolt-fitting is unequivocal. The assembly-line worker should be dissatisfied because he is unable to remove equivocality from his informational input, and no increase in effort will enable him to do so.

There is an interesting ramification of this analysis. The same bolt-fitting operation might produce a marked upswing in satisfaction *if* the operation removed a more substantial portion of equivocality. If, for example, the three bolts affixed some visible feature of an automobile to the frame (e.g., steering column, seats, bumper), then our prediction would be that satisfaction would be higher. It is not the operation of bolting *per se* that determines satisfaction, it is the amount of equivocality that the operation removes. It should be possible to find along an assembly line several workers performing virtually the same operation, but varying in the amount of equivocality they remove. The more equivocality removed, the greater the worker's satisfaction should be, even though they all perform the same operation. Normally, one would assume that similar operations would produce similar amounts of satisfaction. What has been added here is the possibility that this holds true only if the operations remove similar amounts of equivocality. Our analysis also implies that the worker who inserts three bolts into an indistinct car frame *may* be satisfied *if* the particular portion of the frame on which he works is his "total" environment. If that one portion of the frame is seen as equivocal, and *relative to that portion,* inserting bolts *does* remove equivocality, then the worker's satisfaction should be relatively high.

This illustration provides an opportunity to make explicit once more the fact that it is the state of information and *not* the contents *per se* that is important. The system operates on and is controlled by states of information rather than specific contents. In this sense the car frame when it reaches the bolter is no different from the budget memo when it reaches the president's desk. Both contain some equivocality; this equivocality is modified; and the modification is then passed along to some other person. It is in this sense that it is possiule to compare assignments within the same organization and across organizations of widely varying size.

Decision-Making

Decision-making looks quite different when viewed within the organizing model. Although it is tempting to say simply that the model includes decision-making and places it in the selection process, the model implies more than this.

The model implies that the decision-making which occurs in the selection process is *not* the most important decision-making in the system. The crucial decisions are those that pertain to information stored in the retention process. Even though these latter decisions may be made at "lower" levels in the organization, they remain the most crucial ones. They determine the fate of the organization in a way that decisions in the selection process itself do not.

Even if we confine our attention to the selection process, additional changes in the conventional method of handling decision-making become apparent. For decision-making to occur, there must first be accurate registering of the equivocality present in the information that is to be decided about. Little attention has been given to how this information is registered. The present analysis states that the way in which registration occurs will influence the way in which the decision is made. It will be recalled that an inverse relationship exists between the number of rules used to compose the process and the number of cycles that are applied to the information. The more extensive the rules, the fewer the cycles assembled. Translated into the language of decision-making, the relationship would read: the greater the number of rules used to assemble the decision-making process, the fewer the decision premises that will be included in the process. This means that the adequacy of any decision (the amount of equivocality it removes) is extremely variable, and is under the control of the rules for assembling the process and the number of premises that are assembled. It is not necessarily true that past experience is the principal guideline for decision-making, or that decisions are satisfactory rather than optimal. All of these possibilities are secondary to the fact that the state of the informational input controls the form, workings, and output of the process.

Planning

As noted earlier, many organization theorists assume that organizations are rational arrangements of people and props which are held together by plans. This is the traditional emphasis that is most strongly called into question by our model. An example of the emphasis on planning can be seen in the following sentence: "Another contributor to *ineffective* [italics added] performance is the failure of most groups to organize or plan their attack on the problem" (Hoffman, 1965, p. 110). Our view of planning is that it can best be understood as thinking in the future perfect tense. It isn't the plan that gives coherence to actions. Coherence comes from the fact that when the act to be accomplished is projected in the future perfect tense, the means for accomplishing the act become explicit, and the actions run off with greater coherence. It is the reflective glance, *not* the plan *per se,* that permits the act to be accomplished in an orderly way. A plan works because it can be referred *back* to analogous actions in the past, not because it accurately anticipates future contingencies. It is the particular form of reflection produced by the plan, and *not* the particular form of anticipation, that accounts for its failure or success. Plans vary in the clarity with which they enable the actor to review and throw into relief his *lived* experiences. The important property of a plan is the way in which it determines how one views the past.

Even "planned" actions have, at most, only partial orderliness. Plans seem to exist in a context of justification more than in a context of anticipation. They refer more to what has been accomplished than to what is yet to be accomplished. This is why we have argued that it is not surprising that planned actions resemble unplanned actions. There really is no essential difference between these two forms of action at the time of their occurrence. Until they have occurred, actions embedded in a flow of experience are meaningless. It is only when they are singled out reflectively that they become meaningful, coherent, and discrete. Any plan is either phrased in terms of something one has done before or else it is meaningless. If there exists a truly novel situation, one for which there is no analogous experience in the past, then the only thing the person can do is act, so that he can discover what he has done. Actions never performed can hardly be made meaningful, since one has no idea what they are. They simply are performed and *then* made sensible; they *then* appear to be under the control of the plan. At the time of their emission no such control was present. Only after they came to pass was it possible for the actor to say what they were all about.

Managers are frequently advised to construct "better" plans and to do so more often. These prescriptions can be wasteful and misleading. It is wasteful to spend time trying to anticipate future contingencies, because one can never know how things will turn out. If, instead, actions were taken which then could be viewed reflectively and made sensible, there is a greater likelihood that efficiency would improve. This may be one of the reasons why random trial and error, a seemingly inefficient procedure, typically produces results: it generates data that can be viewed reflectively and made meaningful.

Postponing action while planning continues could prove dangerous. If action is postponed, meaning will be postponed, and any chance of clarifying the situation will decrease, simply because there is nothing available to be clarified or made meaningful. Since there is no concrete datum to which reflective attention can be directed (other than the activity of planning itself), there is the distinct possibility that planning could spiral larger and larger, becoming an end rather than a means. Admittedly, we have portrayed an extreme state of affairs. The point is simply that planning can insulate members from the very environment which they are trying to cope with. Planning in the absence of action is basically unconstrained; the only actions available for reflective attention are the planning acts themselves. The members can learn more and more about how to plan and how they are planning, but they can lose sight of what they were originally planning for.

Participative Decision-Making

Organization theory is often more prescriptive than descriptive. This is evident in the extensive discussions of "human relations" (e.g., Argyris, 1964; Bass, 1967a; McGregor, 1967; Sayles, 1963) and, in particular, in the emphasis on participation and power equalization as the means to gain greater acceptance of decisions that affect organizational members. The present view of organizing contains numerous implications for these issues, only a few of which can be sketched here.

An important point for issues of human relations is implicit in the evolutionary model, particularly in the notion of ambivalence. The material presented so far implies that ambivalence is inevitable if organizing is to be accomplished. Opposed tendencies have been mentioned repeatedly (e.g., preserving versus counteracting retained content; registering versus removing equivocality; dissolving versus retaining process structure), and the point has been made repeatedly that they must be preserved if the system is to survive. Campbell (1965a, pp. 304-305) demonstrates the necessity for a system to preserve opposed tendencies in the interest of adaptation, and does so in terms of the opposition between altruistic and selfish motives in humans (see p. 11 where Simmel's view of this opposition was discussed):

> If man has altruistic motives, these are certainly mixed with the purely selfish. . . . [T]here is selection both of tendencies leading one man to survive at the expense of another fellow ingroup member as well as tendencies leading one group to survive at the expense of another group. This dual selective system gets ensconced in man as a fundamental ambivalence between egoism and altruism.

In other words, *both* of the opposed tendencies have survival relevance, and if the organism and group are to survive *both* must be retained. This means that alternate expression of these opposed tendencies will be more adaptive than will an intermediate or compromise expression. This point is of vital importance. Whenever a compromise response is emitted, the adaptive value of the original responses is destroyed. In the example mentioned by Campbell, a response that is partly altruistic and partly selfish furthers *neither* individual nor group survival. The startling fact is that compromise responses are more apt to be selected, since they give the *appearance* of being acceptable to competing interests. The fact of acceptability is not what is crucial here. The crucial point is that, in effecting the compromise solution, important adaptive responses have been selected against and non-adaptive, moderate responses preserved. Should it become necessary in a changed environment for the group to ward off threats to its integrity, or should it become necessary for the individual to defend his own integrity, the crucial responses would be unavailable, since only composites have been retained.

The relevance of this point for participative decision-making is that gaining acceptance through participation may destroy the polarized responses that aid adaptation. A decision that satisfies both group and individual interests selects against a "pure" expression of either of these interests. Should these interests prove to be adaptive in "pure" form, given a change in the environment, then survival becomes problematic.

There is the further point that participation is usually prescribed as a remedy when there is conflict, frustration, and vacillation present in a group. In other words, the expression of ambivalence in a group often triggers a resort to participative techniques. But these practices may well destroy the group's adaptive resources. No one questions the fact that if left on its own the group could destroy itself with conflict and ambivalence. Our point is that the presence of conflict does not necessarily indicate that a group is dissolving; it merely signifies that the group retains heterogeneous responses and preferences, all of which may be adaptive under some circumstances. But, more importantly, if the conflict appears to be destroying the group, then conflict resolution must preserve rather than destroy the polarities exhibited in the conflict. A solution that permits alternate expression of polarized responses would be more adaptive than one that produces compromise responses.

Ambivalence is interesting from yet another perspective. Many organization theorists adopt some form of exchange model as their basic unit of analysis. The present model uses the idea of exchange in its concept of interlocked behaviors. What is interesting about an exchange relationship is that it permits the participants to express opposed tendencies in relatively pure form. To characterize exchange as a situation of maximum interdependence may be missing a crucial point. What exchange actually does is allow each member to express both dependence and independence in relatively pure form. He is able to alternate, within the exchange relationship, between individuated and socialized action, between altruistic and selfish motives. The person is independent when he initiates an action; he is dependent when he responds to the action of another. The argument could be extended. The more the exchange relationship allows a single actor to express both independence and dependence, the greater his involvement in the relationship. This means that as this alternation is rendered less possible, as the distinction between acting independently and dependently is blurred, there should be less satisfaction with the relationship. If dissatisfaction occurs, we should expect to see either a dissolving of the relationship or increased pressure to reinstate the alternation of dependence and independence. Stated in another way, a dyad in which members cooperate should be *less* satisfying than a dyad in which they alternate between cooperation (socialized action) and competition (individuated action). This position is clearly relevant to participation and human relations, since both place more emphasis on the development of cooperation than on the development of competition. Our position would suggest that greater involvement would occur in those situations where members were helped equally to compete and to cooperate.

To summarize our argument, overt conflict is frequently the way in which ambivalent dispositions are expressed. In multiple contingency environments, responses that are appropriate at one point in time may be detrimental at another. Flexibility to deal with environmental changes is maintained if opposed responses are preserved. If conflict is resolved in such a way that compromise responses replace polarized responses, the ability of the group to adapt to its circumstances may well be sacrificed in the interest of group harmony.

Summary

The purpose of this discussion has been to illustrate how supposedly "settled" issues and concepts become unsettled when reviewed in light of the material that has been developed. Attention is directed to "out of the way" places in the organization, and current practices come under closer scrutiny. Although the model of organizing has been stated at an abstract level, when directed at concrete distinctions and prevailing concepts, it does generate a particular way of thinking.

IMPLICATIONS FOR PRACTICE

Although this section is inconsistent with the point made above that organization theory is overprescriptive and underdescriptive, we will go ahead and state some implications for practice that would hold *if* the proposed model is verified to any degree. These suggestions are pure hunches and nothing more. This book has been directed toward the question of how to think about organizations and organizing, not the practical question of how to run an organization. But now, throwing care to the wind, we will point out several practical considerations.

1. *Don't panic in the face of disorder.* This truism takes on considerable importance if the preceding arguments have any validity. Organizations are viewed by members and observers as presumably rational and orderly. When disorder occurs, it is easy to assume that the organization is dissolving. But the preceding suggests that this is not necessarily so. It is necessary for processes to become disorderly if the disorder in information is to be registered accurately. Unless the disorder in information *is* registered accurately, only a small portion of the disorder can be removed, and problems are more likely to increase than decrease. One might assume that adaptation is promoted by an orderly, tightly run organization. If this assumption is made, then ambivalence would be seen as a threat to adaptation. But if the preceding arguments have any merit, precisely the opposite is true. Short-term ambivalence may guarantee long-term adaptation. If some faction of the organization wants to act on the basis of past wisdom, and some other faction wants to act in ways that oppose the past, *both* factions are partially correct. More importantly, both factions should act out their beliefs. This is merely another instance of the split decision pattern that allows the organization to retain both flexibility and stability.

2. *You never do one thing all at once.* One of the practical recommendations that comes from systems theory is that a person can never do one thing (e.g., Hardin, 1963, p. 80). This has been known for some time. In a highly interdependent system, any action ramifies and has far-reaching consequences (e.g., Coser, 1966; Oeser and Harary, 1962; Ring, 1964). What is less commonly asserted is the equally valid point that all of these consequences don't happen at the same time. Some are immediate, some are delayed.

The implications of this are substantial. If a system maintains an odd number of negative cycles (see p. 85), then any change, no matter what it is, will eventually be controlled; the system can dissolve its own disruptions. Any artificial intervention to handle a disruption could destroy the control relationships within the system. And if these control relationships were destroyed, a host of new disruptions would occur. It is possible that a well-functioning control system could be destroyed in the interest of handling a momentary disruption, a disruption that eventually would be dissolved anyway because of the pattern of relationships within the system. The danger of inappropriate intervention is especially likely if members mistakenly assume that people, rather than relationships, are the critical control points in an organization.

There is a very different implication of the point about consequences ramifying. Since a given event can ramify and have multiple effects, whenever a problem is perceived, caution must be exercised in determining its origin. In a highly interdependent system, it is likely that the origin of the problem will be at some distance from the symptom. While it may be true that people tend to search in the "vicinity of the problem for its cause," in the case of interdependent systems this form of search may be wasteful and lead to inaccurate diagnoses.

3. *Chaotic action is preferable to orderly inaction.* The discussions of planning (pp. 101-103) and the enacted environment emphasized that meaning is retrospective, and only elapsed experience is available for meaningful interpretation. The practical implication is that an organization would be in a better position to improve its efficiency if the elapsed experience were filled with action rather than inaction. Action, when viewed retrospectively, clarifies what the organization is doing and what its projects may be. Inaction, viewed retrospectively, is more difficult to render meaningful: there is a greater likelihood for irrelevant meanings to be attached and for a state of autistic thinking to develop. Actions, in other words, provide tangible items that can be attended to. In the absence of actions, the reflective gaze is directed toward relatively unfilled periods of lived experience; in order to find some meaning, it will probably push farther back in time and light on past experience that occurred some time ago. Reflection is not exquisitely sensitive to degrees of pastness; what is past is past. Immediate and remote past are difficult to distinguish. This being the case, if the immediate past is not filled with action which engages the reflective glance, then the remote past may be mistaken for the recent past. And if distant experiences are revived, recreated, and made meaningful, then the meaning of any present circumstance is really an ancient meaning. This could reduce the chance for the system to adapt to present contingencies.

When a group is without a project and is confused, the emission of actions which can be viewed reflectively increases the chances that the group may discover what it is doing. But in the absence of action, there is little chance to clarify the confusion. Thus, when there is confusion in a group, and some member asks, "What should I do?" and some other member says, "I don't know, just *do something*," that is probably a much better recommendation than one might realize. It is better for the simple reason that it increases the likelihood that something will be generated which can then be made meaningful.

4. *The most important decisions are often the least apparent.* This point is a restatement of the idea that decisions made in the selection process have less to do with the fate of a system than do the decisions made concerning retention. This means that the retention process and the persons who mediate between it and the selection and enactment processes are the most crucial points in terms of organizing. The person who makes decisions about what the goal of the company should be next year is less important to continued functioning than is the person(s) who decides what is known by the company, what should be done next in terms of selection and enactment, and whether opposing decisions are made for selection and enactment. The company historian in a very real sense is also the company prophet. Knowing what will be done about the company history, he can

state with accuracy what the fate of the system will be; for unless one of the processes within the company is permitted to counteract the history and the other to preserve it, destruction is likely.

5.   *You should coordinate processes rather than groups.* The way in which an organization functions depends on the relationships that exist among processes rather than among groups. It is easy to mistake groups for distinct processes; however, to coordinate the organization, you need to locate the processes of enactment, selection, and retention, determine the direction of the causal ties among them, and then adjust the causal linkages so that you have an odd number of negative cycles. Groups are important because they house and assemble processes, and pass information to other processes. The actions performed by a group are less important than are the processes they perform, the other processes they are related to, and the directions of those relationships. It is the direct or indirect causal linkages, not the particular functionings of particular groups, that are crucial to the continued functioning of the organization. The control network that exists at the system (organization) level determines the functioning of the system, and this network comprises relationships among processes, not among groups.

Admittedly, these five illustrations only hint at ways in which practice might be altered in terms of the concepts developed in this book. At this stage hints are the best we can do. The important thing is to determine the accuracy of the concepts, so that more definite implications for practice can be drawn. In the meantime, we may be content in the thought that if there is any validity to the model, if it has any relation to everyday life, then people already are acting somewhat in the way it suggests, even if they are not doing so self-consciously.

CONCLUSION

Having started this book with a grook, it seems appropriate to end with one:

> Our choicest plans
>   have fallen through.
> Our airiest castles
>   tumbled over,
> because of lines
>   we neatly drew
> and later neatly
>   stumbled over.[2]

[2]From Piet Hein, *Grooks* (Cambridge, Mass.: M.I.T. Press, 1966), p. 17. Reprinted by permission.

Existing theories of organization draw lines that mark off some of the supposed contours of formal organizations. Some of these lines we have honored; others we have erased. In place of those lines that we erased, we have drawn other ones. It is inevitable that people will stumble over these new lines in new ways. The best we can hope for is that, having fallen flat on their faces, people will look more closely at the ground beneath them.

References

Abt Associates (1965). *Survey of the state of the art: social, political and economic models and simulations.* Cambridge, Mass.: Abt Associates Inc.

Allport, F. H. (1924). *Social psychology.* Cambridge, Mass.: Houghton Mifflin.

Allport, F. H. (1955). *Theories of perception and the concept of structure.* New York: Wiley.

Allport, F. H. (1962). A structuronomic conception of behavior: individual and collective. *Journal of Abnormal and Social Psychology, 64,* 3-30.

Allport, F. H. (1967). A theory of enestruence (event-structure theory): report of progress. *American Psychologist, 22,* 1-24.

Allport, G. W. (1961). *Pattern and growth in personality.* New York: Holt, Rinehart and Winston.

Altman, I. (1966). Aspects of the criterion problem in small group research. II. The analysis of group tasks. *Acta Psychologica, 25,* 199-221.

Argyris, C. (1964). *Integrating the individual and the organization.* New York: Wiley.

Asch, S. E. (1952). *Social psychology.* Englewood Cliffs, N. J.: Prentice-Hall.

Ashby, W. R. (1956). *An introduction to cybernetics.* New York: Wiley.

Ashby, W. R. (1962). Principles of the self-organizing system. In H. Von Foerster and G. W. Zopf (Eds.), *Principles of self-organization.* New York: Pergamon Press. Pp. 255-278.

Atkinson, J. W., and D. Cartwright (1964). Some neglected variables in contemporary conceptions of decision and performance. *Psychological Reports, 14,* 575-590.

Bales, R. F. (1950). *Interaction process analysis.* Reading, Mass.: Addison-Wesley.

Bales, R. F., and F. L. Strodtbeck (1951). Phases in group problem solving. *Journal of Abnormal and Social Psychology, 46,* 485-495.

Barker, R. G., and H. F. Wright (1955). *Midwest and its children.* Evanston, Ill.: Row-Peterson.

Barnard, C. I. (1938). *The functions of the executive.* Cambridge, Mass.: Harvard Univ. Press.

Barnard, C. I. (1948). *Organization and management.* Cambridge, Mass.: Harvard Univ. Press.

Barnes, L. B. (1960). *Organizational systems and engineering groups.* Cambridge, Mass.: Harvard Univ. Press.

Bass, B. M. (1967a). The anarchist movement and the T group: some possible lessons for organization development. *Applied Behavioral Science, 3,* 211-239.

Bass, B. M. (1967b). How to succeed in business according to business students and managers. Technical Report 15. Management Research Center, University of Pittsburgh.

Bass, B. M., and G. Dunteman (1963). Biases in the evaluation of one's own group, its allies and opponents. *Journal of Conflict Resolution, 7,* 16-20.

Bem, D. J. (1965). An experimental analysis of self-persuasion. *Journal of Experimental Social Psychology, 1,* 199-218.

Bem, D. J. (1967). Self-perception: the dependent variable of human performance. *Organizational Behavior and Human Performance, 2,* 105-121.

Bennis, W. G. (1959). Leadership theory and administrative behavior: the problem of authority. *Administrative Science Quarterly, 4,* 259-301.

Bertalanffy, L. von (1967). *Robots, men, and minds.* New York: Braziller.

Blau, P. M. (1954). Patterns of interaction among a group of officials in a government agency. *Human Relations, 7,* 337-348.

Blau, P. M. (1959). Social integration, social rank, and processes of interaction. *Human Organization, 18* (4), 152-157.

Blau, P. M. (1964). *Exchange and power in social life.* New York: Wiley.

Blauner, R. (1960). Work satisfaction and industrial trends in modern society. In W. Galenson and S. M. Lipset (Eds.), *Labor and trade unionism.* New York: Wiley. Pp. 339-360.

Bradney, Pamela (1957). Quasi-familial relationships in industry. *Human Relations, 10,* 271-278.

Brehm, J. W., and A. R. Cohen (1962). *Explorations in cognitive dissonance.* New York: Wiley.

Bridgman, P. W. (1959). *The way things are.* Cambridge, Mass.: Harvard Univ. Press.

Broadbent, D. E. (1958). *Perception and communication.* New York: Pergamon Press.

Brodbeck, May (1958). Methodological individualisms: definition and reduction. *Philosophy of Science, 25,* 1-22.

Byrne, D., and G. L. Clore (1967). Effectance arousal and attraction. *Journal of Personality and Social Psychology, 6* (4), Whole No. 638. Monogr. Suppl.

Campbell, D. T. (1958). Systematic error on the part of human links in communication systems. *Information and Control, 1,* 334-369.

Campbell, D. T. (1959). Methodological suggestions from a comparative psychology of knowledge processes. *Inquiry, 2,* 152-182.

Campbell, D. T. (1961). Conformity in psychology's theories of acquired behavioral dispositions. In I. A. Berg and B. M. Bass (Eds.), *Conformity and deviation.* New York: Harper. Pp. 101-142.

Campbell, D. T. (1963). Social attitudes and other acquired behavioral dispositions. In S. Koch (Ed.), *Psychology: a study of a science.* Vol. 6. New York: McGraw-Hill. Pp. 94-172.

Campbell, D. T. (1965a). Ethnocentric and other altruistic motives. In D. Levine (Ed.), *Nebraska symposium on motivation, 1965.* Lincoln: Univ. of Nebraska Press. Pp. 283-311.

Campbell, D. T. (1965b). Variation and selective retention in socio-cultural evolution. In H. R. Barringer, G. I. Blanksten, and R. Mack (Eds.), *Social change in developing areas.* Cambridge, Mass.: Schenkman. Pp. 19-49.

Campbell, D. T. (1967). Stereotypes and the perception of group differences. *American Psychologist, 22,* 817-829.

Caplow, T. (1964). *Principles of organization.* New York: Harcourt, Brace and World.

Carey, A. (1967). The Hawthorne studies: a radical criticism. *American Sociological Review, 32,* 403-416.

Carzo, R., and J. N. Yanouzas (1967). *Formal organization: a systems approach.* Homewood, Ill.: Irwin-Dorsey.

Cofer, C. N., and M. H. Appley (1964). *Motivation: theory and research.* New York: Wiley.

Cohen, A. M., and W. G. Bennis (1961). Continuity of leadership in communication networks. *Human Relations, 14,* 351-367.

Cohen, A. M., W. G. Bennis, and G. H. Wolkon (1962). The effects of changes in communication networks on the behaviors of problem-solving groups. *Sociometry, 25,* 177-196.

Coser, Rose L. (1966). Role distance, sociological ambivalence, and transitional status systems. *American Journal of Sociology, 72,* 173-187.

Costello, T. S., and S. S. Zalkind (1963). *Psychology in administration: a research orientation.* Englewood Cliffs, N. J.: Prentice-Hall.

Cyert, R. M., and J. G. March (1963). *A behavioral theory of the firm.* Englewood Cliffs, N. J.: Prentice-Hall.

Deutsch, M. (1949). A theory of cooperation and competition. *Human Relations, 2,* 129-152.

Drabek, T. E., and J. E. Haas (1967). Realism in laboratory simulation: myth or method? *Social Forces, 45,* 337-346.

Dubin, R. (1962). Business behavior behaviorally viewed. In C. Argyris *et al., Social science approaches to business behavior.* Homewood, Ill.: Dorsey Press. Pp. 11-55.

Etzioni, A. (1964). *Modern organizations.* Englewood Cliffs, N. J.: Prentice-Hall.

Evan, W. M. (1963). Indices of the hierarchical structure of industrial organizations. *Management Science, 9,* 468-477.

Faucheux, C., and K. D. Mackenzie (1966). Task dependency of organizational centrality: its behavioral consequences. *Journal of Experimental Social Psychology, 2,* 361-375.

Festinger, L. (1954). A theory of social comparison processes. *Human Relations, 7,* 117-140.

Festinger, L. (1957). *A theory of cognitive dissonance.* Evanston, Ill.: Row, Peterson.

Festinger, L., S. Schachter, and K. Back (1950). *Social pressures in informal groups: a study of a housing project.* New York: Harper.

Friedmann, G. (1954). Outline for a psycho-sociology of assembly line work. *Human Organization, 13* (4), 15-20.

Garfinkel, H. (1963). A conception of, and experiments with, "trust" as a condition of stable concerted actions. In O. J. Harvey (Ed.), *Motivation and social interaction.* New York: Ronald Press. Pp. 187-238.

Garfinkel, H. (1967). *Studies of ethnomethodology.* Englewood Cliffs, N. J.: Prentice-Hall.

Garfinkel, H. (1968). Ethnomethodology and everyday life. Talk presented at The Ohio State University, April 1968.

Gartner, Dorothy, and M. A. Iverson (1967). Some effects of upward mobile status in established and ad hoc groups. *Journal of Personality and Social Psychology, 5,* 390-397.

Glasser, W. (1965). *Reality therapy.* New York: Harper and Row.

Guetzkow, H. (1961). Organizational leadership in task-oriented groups. In L. Petrullo and B. M. Bass (Eds.), *Leadership and interpersonal behavior.* New York: Holt, Rinehart and Winston. Pp. 187-200.

Guetzkow, H. (1962). Joining field and laboratory work in disaster research. In G. W. Baker and D. W. Chapman (Eds.), *Man and society in disaster.* New York: Basic Books. Pp. 337-355.

Guetzkow, H. (1968). Some correspondences between simulations and "realities" in international relations. In M. Kaplan (Ed.), *New approaches to international relations*. New York: St. Martin's Press.

Hackman, J. R. (in press). Tasks and task performance in research on stress. In J. E. McGrath (Ed.), *Social and psychological factors in stress*. New York: Holt, Rinehart and Winston.

Hall, J., and Martha S. Williams (1966). A comparison of decision-making performances in established and ad hoc groups. *Journal of Personality and Social Psychology, 3,* 214-222.

Hall, R. L. (1957). Group performance under feedback that confounds responses of group members. *Sociometry, 20,* 297-305.

Hardin, G. (1963). The cybernetics of competition: a biologist's view of society. *Perspectives in biology and medicine, 7,* 61-84.

Heider, F. (1958). *The psychology of interpersonal relations*. New York: Wiley.

Hein, P. (1966). *Grooks*. Cambridge, Mass.: M.I.T. Press.

Heiskanen, I. (1967). *Theoretical approaches and scientific strategies in administrative and organizational research. A methodological study*. Helsinki: Helsingfors.

Hoffman, L. R. (1965). Group problem solving. In L. Berkowitz (Ed.), *Advances in experimental social psychology*. Vol. 2. New York: Academic Press. Pp. 99-132.

Hollander, E. P., and R. H. Willis (1967). Some current issues in the psychology of conformity and nonconformity. *Psychological Bulletin, 68,* 62-76.

Homans, G. C. (1958). Social behavior as exchange. *American Journal of Sociology, 63,* 597-606.

Homans, G. C. (1961). *Social behavior: its elementary forms*. New York: Harcourt, Brace.

Indik, B. P. (1963). Some effects of organization size on member attitudes and behavior. *Human Relations, 16,* 369-384.

Jones, E. E., and H. Gerard (1967). *Foundations of social psychology*. New York: Wiley.

Kahn, R. L., D. M. Wolfe, R. P. Quinn, J. D. Snoek, and R. A. Rosenthal (1964). *Organizational stress*. New York: Wiley.

Katz, D. (1964). The motivational basis of organizational behavior. *Behavioral Science, 9,* 131-146.

Katz, D., and R. L. Kahn (1966). *The social psychology of organizations*. New York: Wiley.

Katz, D., and E. Stotland (1959). A preliminary statement to a theory of attitude structure and change. In S. Koch (Ed.), *Psychology: a study of a science*. Vol. 3. New York: McGraw-Hill. Pp. 423-475.

Kelley, H. H., J. W. Thibaut, R. Radloff, and O. Mundy (1962). The development of cooperation in the "minimal social situation." *Psychological Monographs, 76* (19), Whole No. 538.

Krech, D. (1968). Titchener on experimental psychology. *American Psychologist, 23*, 367-368.

LaBarre, W. (1968). Personality from a psychoanalytic viewpoint. In E. Norbeck, D. Price-Williams, and W. McCord (Eds.), *The study of personality.* New York: Holt, Rinehart and Winston. Pp. 65-87.

Latane, H. A. (1963). The rationality model in organizational decision-making. In H. J. Leavitt (Ed.), *The social science of organizations.* Englewood Cliffs, N. J.: Prentice-Hall. Pp. 87-136.

Lawrence, P. R. (1958). *The changing of organizational behavior patterns.* Cambridge, Mass.: Harvard Univ. Press.

Lazarus, R. S. (1966). *Psychological stress and the coping process.* New York: McGraw-Hill.

Lewis, L. S., and D. Brissett (1967). Sex as work: a study of avocational counseling. *Social Problems, 15*, 8-18.

Likert, R. (1961). *New patterns of management.* New York: McGraw-Hill.

Longabaugh, R. (1966). The structure of interpersonal behavior. *Sociometry, 29*, 441-460.

Lorge, I., D. Fox, J. Davitz, and M. Brenner (1958). A survey of studies contrasting the quality of group performance and individual performance, 1920-1957. *Psychological Bulletin, 55*, 337-372.

Lott, A. J., and B. E. Lott (1965). Group cohesiveness as interpersonal attraction: a review of relationships with antecedent and consequent variables. *Psychological Bulletin, 64*, 259-309.

Lowin, A., and J. R. Craig (1968). The influence of level of performance on managerial style: an experimental object-lesson in the ambiguity of correlational data. *Organizational Behavior and Human Performance, 3*, 440-458.

Lundberg, C. C. (1968). Toward understanding behavioral science by administrators. In D. R. Hampton (Ed.), *Behavioral concepts in management.* Belmont, Calif.: Dickenson. Pp. 69-83.

McGregor, D. (1960). *The human side of enterprise.* New York: McGraw-Hill.

McGregor, D. (1967). *The professional manager.* New York: McGraw-Hill.

MacKay, D. M. (1968). Towards an information-flow model of human behavior. In W. R. Buckley (Ed.), *Modern systems research for the behavioral scientist.* Chicago: Aldine. Pp. 359-368.

Mackenzie, K. D. (1967). Decomposition of communication networks. *Journal of Mathematical Psychology, 4*, 162-174.

McLachlan, D. (1961). Communication networks and monitoring. *Public Opinion Quarterly, 25*, 194-209.

Maier, N. R. F. (1950). The quality of group decisions as influenced by the discussion leader. *Human Relations, 3,* 155-174.

Maier, N. R. F. (1963). *Problem-solving discussions and conferences: leadership methods and skills.* New York: McGraw-Hill.

Maier, N. R. F., and L. R. Hoffman (1960). Quality of first and second solutions in group problem solving. *Journal of Applied Psychology, 44,* 278-283.

Maier, N. R. F., and A. R. Solem (1962). Improving solutions by turning choice situations into problems. *Personnel Psychology, 15,* 151-157.

Mandler, G. (1964). The interruption of behavior. In D. Levine (Ed.), *Nebraska symposium on motivation, 1964.* Lincoln: Univ. of Nebraska Press. Pp. 163-219.

March, J. G., and H. A. Simon (1958). *Organizations.* New York: Wiley.

Maruyama, M. (1963). The second cybernetics: deviation-amplifying mutual causal processes. *American Scientist, 51,* 164-179.

Mead, G. H. (1956). *Social psychology* (ed. A. Strauss). Chicago: Univ. of Chicago Press.

Mead, Margaret (1963). The pattern of leisure in contemporary American culture. In H. M. Ruitenbeek (Ed.), *The dilemma of organizational society.* New York: Dutton. Pp. 177-185.

Mechanic, D. (1964). Sources of power of lower participants in complex organizations. In W. W. Cooper, H. J. Leavitt, and M. W. Shelly (Eds.), *New perspectives in organization research.* New York: Wiley. Pp. 136-149.

Merleau-Ponty, M. (1963). *The structure of behavior.* Boston: Beacon Press.

Merton, R. K. (1940). Bureaucratic structure and personality. *Social Forces, 18,* 560-568.

Merton, R. K. (1963). Basic research and potentials of relevance. *American Behavioral Scientist, 6* (9), 86-90.

Miller, G. A., E. Galanter, and K. H. Pribram (1960). *Plans and the structure of behavior.* New York: Holt, Rinehart and Winston.

Miller, L. K., and R. L. Hamblin (1963). Interdependence, differential rewarding, and productivity. *American Sociological Review, 28,* 768-778.

Mills, C. W. (1966). *Sociology and pragmatism.* New York: Oxford.

Mills, T. M. (1967). *The sociology of small groups.* Englewood Cliffs, N. J.: Prentice-Hall.

Morris, C. G. (1966). Task effects on group interaction. *Journal of Personality and Social Psychology, 4,* 545-554.

Newcomb, T. M. (1956). The prediction of interpersonal attraction. *American Psychologist, 11,* 575-586.

Newcomb, T. M. (1961). *The acquaintance process.* New York: Holt, Rinehart and Winston.

Newcomb, T. M., R. H. Turner, and P. E. Converse (1965). *Social Psychology*. New York: Holt, Rinehart and Winston.

O'Connell, J. J. (1968). *Managing organizational innovation*. Homewood, Ill.: Irwin.

Oeser, O. A., and F. Harary (1962). A mathematical model for structural role theory. I. *Human Relations, 15,* 89-109.

Ogburn, W. F. (1922). *Social change*. New York: Viking Press.

Opsahl, R. L., and M. D. Dunnette (1966). The role of financial compensation in industrial motivation. *Psychological Bulletin, 66,* 94-118.

Osborn, A. F. (1953). *Applied imagination*. New York: Scribners.

Pepinsky, H. B., K. E. Weick, and J. W. Riner (1965). *Primer for productivity*. Columbus, Ohio: Ohio State University Research Foundation.

Perrow, C. (1967). A framework for the comparative analysis of organizations. *American Sociological Review, 32,* 194-208.

Porter, L. W., and E. E. Lawler (1965). Properties of organization structure in relation to job attitudes and job behavior. *Psychological Bulletin, 64,* 23-51.

Pugh, D. S. (1966). Modern organization theory. *Psychological Bulletin, 66,* 235-251.

Rabinowitz, L., H. H. Kelley, and R. M. Rosenblatt (1966). Effects of different types of interdependence and response conditions in the minimal social situation. *Journal of Experimental Social Psychology, 2,* 169-197.

Rapoport, A. (1953). What is information? *ETC, 10,* 247-260.

Read, W. H. (1962). Upward communication in industrial hierarchies. *Human Relations, 15,* 3-15.

Riecken, H. W., and G. C. Homans (1954). Psychological aspects of social structure. In G. Lindzey (Ed.), *Handbook of social psychology*. Vol. 2. Cambridge, Mass.: Addison-Wesley. Pp. 786-832.

Riesman, D., R. J. Potter, and Jeanne Watson (1960). Sociability, permissiveness, and equality. *Psychiatry, 23,* 323-340.

Ring, K. (1964). Some determinants of interpersonal attraction in hierarchical relationships. *Journal of Personality, 32,* 651-665.

Roby, T. B. (1966). Self-enacting response sequences and reinforcement: conjecture. *Psychological Reports, 19,* 19-31.

Roethlisberger, F. J., and W. Dickson (1939). *Management and the worker*. Cambridge: Harvard Univ. Press.

Rohde, K. J. (1967). Effect of early experience on the child: possible solution to controversy. *Psychological Reports, 20,* 134.

Rokeach, M. (1961). Authority, authoritarianism, and conformity. In I. A. Berg and B. M. Bass (Eds.), *Conformity and deviation* New York: Harper. Pp. 230-257.

Rokeach, M. (1966). Attitude change and behavioral change. *Public Opinion Quarterly, 30,* 529-550.

Sayles, L. R. (1963). *Individualism and big business.* New York: McGraw-Hill.

Schachter, S. (1967). Cognitive effects on bodily functioning: studies of obesity and eating. In D. C. Glass (Ed.), *Neurophysiology and emotion.* New York: Rockefeller Univ. Press. Pp. 117-144.

Schein, E. H. (1965). *Organizational psychology.* Englewood Cliffs, N. J.: Prentice-Hall.

Schneirla, T. C. (1959). An evolutionary and developmental theory of biphasic processes underlying approach and withdrawal. In M. R. Jones (Ed.), *Nebraska symposium on motivation, 1959.* Lincoln: Univ. of Nebraska Press. Pp. 1-42.

Schramm, W. (1955). Information theory and mass communication. *Journalism Quarterly, 32,* 131-146.

Schutz, A. (1967). *The phenomenology of the social world.* Evanston, Ill.: Northwestern Univ. Press.

Scott, W. A. (1963). Conceptualizing and measuring structural properties of cognition. In O. J. Harvey (Ed.), *Motivation and social interaction.* New York: Ronald Press. Pp. 266-288.

Scott, W. R. (1965). Field methods in the study of organizations. In J. G. March (Ed.), *Handbook of organizations.* Chicago: Rand McNally. Pp. 261-304.

Scott, W. R., S. M. Dornbusch, B. C. Busching, and J. D. Laing (1967). Organizational evaluation and authority. *Administrative Science Quarterly, 12,* 93-117.

Seashore, S. E. (1966). Field experiments with formal organizations. In R. Bowers (Ed.), *Studies on behavior in organizations.* Athens, Ga.: Univ. of Georgia Press. Pp. 87-100.

Shapiro, D., and P. H. Leiderman (1967). Arousal correlates of task role and group setting. *Journal of Personality and Social Psychology, 5,* 103-107.

Shaw, M. E. (1964). Communication networks. In L. Berkowitz (Ed.), *Advances in experimental social psychology.* Vol. 1. New York: Academic Press. Pp. 111-149.

Sherif, M., and Carolyn W. Sherif (1964). *Reference groups.* New York: Harper.

Shure, G. H., M. S. Rogers, Ida M. Larsen, and J. Tassone (1962). Group planning and task effectiveness. *Sociometry, 25,* 263-282.

Sidowski, J. B. (1957). Reward and punishment in a minimal social situation. *Journal of Experimental Psychology, 54,* 318-326.

Simmel, G. (1950). *The sociology of Georg Simmel* (trans. K. H. Wolff). New York: Free Press.

Simon, H. A. (1957). *Administrative behavior.* New York: Free Press.

Skinner, B. F. (1963). Behaviorism at fifty. *Science, 140,* 951-958.

Skinner, B. F. (1966). The phylogeny and ontogeny of behavior. *Science, 153,* 1205-1213.

Slack, C. W. (1955). Feedback theory and the reflex arc concept. *Psychological Review, 62,* 263-267.

Stager, P. (1967). Conceptual level as a composition variable in small-group decision-making. *Journal of Personality and Social Psychology, 5,* 152-161.

Steiner, I. D. (1955). Interpersonal behavior as influenced by accuracy of social perception. *Psychological Review, 62,* 268-274.

Tannenbaum, A. S. (1968). *Control in organizations.* New York: McGraw-Hill.

Temerlin, M. K. (1963). On choice and responsibility in a humanistic psychotherapy. *Journal of Humanistic Psychology, 3,* 35-48.

Thibaut, J. W., and H. H. Kelley (1959). *The social psychology of groups.* New York: Wiley.

Thompson, J. D. (1967). *Organizations in action.* New York: McGraw-Hill.

Toch, H. (1966). *The social psychology of social movements.* Indianapolis: Bobbs-Merrill.

Tuckman, B. W. (1964). Personality structure, group composition, and group functioning. *Sociometry, 27,* 469-487.

Tuckman, B. W. (1967). Group composition and group performance of structured and unstructured tasks. *Journal of Experimental Social Psychology, 3,* 25-40.

Vinacke, W. E., Doris C. Crowell, Dora Dien, and Vera Young (1966). The effect of information about strategy on a three-person game. *Behavioral Science, 11,* 180-189.

Walker, C. R., and R. H. Guest (1952). The man on the assembly line. *Harvard Business Review, 30* (3), 71-83.

Watzlawick, P., Janet H. Beavin, and D. D. Jackson (1967). *Pragmatics of human communication.* New York: Norton.

Weaver, W. (1949). The mathematics of communication. *Scientific American, 181,* 11-15.

Weick, K. E. (1965). Laboratory experimentation with organizations. In J. G. March (Ed.), *Handbook of organizations.* Chicago: Rand McNally. Pp. 194-260.

Weick, K. E. (1966). Task acceptance dilemmas: a site for research on cognition. In S. Feldman (Ed.), *Cognitive consistency.* New York: Academic Press. Pp. 225-255.

Weick, K. E. (1967). Organizations in the laboratory. In V. H. Vroom (Ed.), *Methods of organizational research.* Pittsburgh: Univ. of Pittsburgh Press. Pp. 1-56.

Weick, K. E. (1968). Systematic observational methods. In G. Lindzey and E. Aronson (Eds.), *The handbook of social psychology* (2nd ed.). Vol. 2. Reading, Mass.: Addison-Wesley.

White, R. W. (1959). Motivation reconsidered: the concept of competence. *Psychological Review, 66,* 297-333.

Whyte, W. F. (1959). *Man and organization.* Homewood, Ill.: Irwin.

Whyte, W. F., and Edith L. Hamilton (1964). *Action research for management.* Homewood, Ill.: Irwin-Dorsey.

Zajonc, R. B. (1965). Social facilitation. *Science, 149,* 269-274.

Zander, A., and D. Wolfe (1964). Administrative rewards and coordination among committee members. *Administrative Science Quarterly, 9,* 50-69.

Ziller, R. C. (1964). Individuation and socialization. *Human Relations, 17,* 341-360.

BCDE79876543210